DIVINE RENOVATION
Guidebook

A Step-by-Step Manual for Transforming Your Parish

FR. JAMES MALLON

Foreword by PATRICK LENCIONI

TWENTY-THIRD PUBLICATIONS

twentythirdpublications.com

NIHIL OBSTAT:
+ Anthony Mancini
ARCHBISHOP OF HALIFAX-YARMOUTH
May 9, 2016

Interior images: courtesy of the author. Used with permission.

Second Printing 2016

TWENTY-THIRD PUBLICATIONS
1 Montauk Avenue, Suite 200, New London, CT 06320
(860) 437-3012 » (800) 321-0411 » www.twentythirdpublications.com

© Copyright 2016 Novalis Publishing, Inc. All rights reserved.
No part of this publication may be reproduced in any manner
without prior written permission of the publisher.
Write to the Permissions Editor.

ISBN: 978-1-62785-224-1

Printed in Canada.

"Everybody wants to belong to a fabulous parish. Fr. James Mallon is one of the most passionate people I know when it comes to helping priests and parishioners transform their parishes into dynamic communities centred on Jesus. This *Divine Renovation Guidebook* is a gem. Too often we talk about these things in theoretical ways that don't translate into the practical reality of parish life. This guidebook is practical and insightful!"

Matthew Kelly, founder of Dynamic Catholic and author of *Rediscover Jesus*

"When I started reading *Divine Renovation* and this new work, *Divine Renovation Guidebook*, I began to tear up. I am so moved by James Mallon's love for the Church. More than that, I have visited his church on a Sunday and seen the evidence of what a divine renovation can do for the lives of people. This book is not only hyper-practical, it will make your heart swell with hope for the Church – the entire Church."

Carey Nieuwhof, author and Pastor, Connexus Church

"I am delighted to recommend Fr. James Mallon's *Divine Renovation Guidebook*. It is an extremely practical resource that offers many excellent tips and exercises to help plan and implement a vision for the transformation of the parish."

Nicky Gumbel, Vicar of Holy Trinity Brompton, London, and pioneer of Alpha

"*Divine Renovation* and this guidebook constitute a unique resource for parishes and dioceses looking into concrete ways of living an effective pastoral conversion. We have trained over 600 priests and bishops on pastoral leadership and are overjoyed that they can use the hugely relevant and practical approach that Fr. James Mallon has generously shared. We can only imagine the huge amount of work this has required and are grateful for the fruit it is already bearing in Europe."

Marc and Florence de Leyritz, executive coaches and co-founders of Des Pasteurs Selon Mon Coeur

"Finally, a very practical book for parishes that feel God is calling them to effectiveness. Fr. Mallon and the team at @SaintBP will help your team walk step by step to move from vision to implementation across a broad cross-section of ministry areas in your parish. Beneficial not only for Catholics but also for Evangelical churches."

Dave Travis, CEO, Leadership Network, the premier network for Evangelical congregations

"We are so grateful for the work and ministry of James Mallon. He knows how to build a growing, healthy parish and is a great guide to any parish interested in doing the same."

(Rev.) Michael White and Tom Corcoran, authors of *Rebuilt*

"For a long time we've been looking for a toolbox to help renew parish life. And now there is one. Fr. Mallon's *Divine Renovation Guidebook* takes the step-by-step approach we need to focus on becoming intentional disciples of Jesus and moving from maintenance to mission in ministry. This workbook is easy to use, extraordinarily practical in the strategies and tips recommended, and infused with a solid Gospel vision. Because it is also chock full of timely and wise suggestions, pithy anecdotes, assessment tools and discussion questions, the *Guidebook* is a superb resource for every 21st-century parish intent on making joyful missionary disciples."

J. Michael Miller, CSB, Archbishop of Vancouver

"If the church is to meet the challenge of ministry in the 21st century, there must be something truly life-giving in the parish, the community where faith is nurtured and Catholics learn to live out their Christian calling. Fr. Mallon's *Divine Renovation Guidebook* will equip readers to transform their parishes into robustly healthy, dynamic centres of evangelization and grace. At once practical and visionary, simple and comprehensive, this guidebook is a terrific resource for all Catholics who want to see their parishes flourish in ways they never dreamed possible."

William E. Simon, Jr., Founder, Parish Catalyst and author of *Great Catholic Parishes: A Living Mosaic*

"In North America, there are priests who pastor parishes and others who write about how to do it. Very few do both. Fr. James Mallon is one of a handful of exceptions – and that is what makes this book so wonderful. You hold in your hand the guidebook of the hard-won insights he and his team have achieved. It is a precious treasure. Use it well and you will see lives transform – including your own!"

Dominic Perri, Lead Consultant, Amazing Parish Movement

"*Divine Renovation Guidebook* is an invaluable problem solver when it comes to building healthy parishes. Fr. Mallon has not only identified the key issues to be addressed, but offers sound answers that will guide parishes into a new dimension of mission. Reading this guidebook brought hope to my heart regarding the future of parishes."

Jeff Cavins, founder of The Great Adventure Bible Study

"With *Divine Renovation*, Fr. Mallon has inspired thousands of pastoral leaders to seek 'missionary conversion' in order to be faithful to Christ's Great Commission to 'go, and make disciples.' This new guidebook marks another great contribution to the New Evangelization with its practical, step-by-step guidance and indispensable tools and resources to help parishes become true centres of evangelization."

Archbishop William E. Lori, Archdiocese of Baltimore

Table of Contents

Foreword *by Patrick Lencioni* **7**

Introduction **9**

Do You Have to Read *Divine Renovation* to Use This Guidebook? **10**

1. The Pastor: It Starts with the Leader **11**
2. The Team: The Pastor Can't Do It Alone **17**
3. The Prep: Being Strategic about Being Strategic **37**
4. The End and the Beginning: Vision and Assessment **55**
5. The Plan: You Need a Vision *and* a Plan **82**
6. The Weekend: The Centrality of the Eucharist **126**
7. The Processes: Replace Programs with Process **151**
8. The People: Staff and Leadership Culture **172**
9. The Sacraments: The Privileged Place of Encounter **189**
10. The World: Expanding Our Vision **209**

Acknowledgements **213**

Appendixes: Resources and Tools

Appendix A: Resources... **215**
Appendix B: Organizations and Ministries... **216**
Appendix C: The Divine Renovation Network.. **217**
Appendix D: Discussion Resources for *Divine Renovation*, Chapter 3: House of Pain **218**
Appendix E: For the Geeks.. **220**

Foreword

A Catholic parish is nothing short of an outpost of the Great Commission. Think about that. When Jesus told his disciples before his Ascension to go to the ends of the earth to share the Gospel, the physical manifestation of that call would be a parish.

Somehow, we Catholics lose sight of that. We think that an outpost for Christ would have to be a church in the middle of the desert in a distant foreign land. That, we may think, is where real missionary work is done. But the reality of the New Evangelization is that most of our parishes, be they in suburbs or urban centres or rural countrysides, are the tip of the spear in a world where people's souls are going drier and drier.

And so, the question that must be asked is this: Is there any reason not to make our parishes the most effective outposts they can be? Or perhaps this is a better question: Is there another kind of organization in the world that is more important and more deserving of higher standards than a parish? The answer to both of these questions must be a resounding 'no'.

The question that remains, and the purpose of the book you are now reading, is "How can I make my parish the most effective outpost of the Great Commission and the New Evangelization?"

Fr. James Mallon spends a lot of his time thinking about and praying about and talking about that very question. He sees the need in the world for Jesus and his Church, and wants every parish to be the best it can be. And Fr. Mallon has tried a lot of things over the years to make the parishes he leads better. Some have worked wonderfully. Others have failed. Now he has taken all that he has learned – and it's a lot – and put it into one big guidebook.

What should you do with this guidebook? Something. Anything. Just get started. Don't get intimidated by all the ideas, and don't wait until the perfect time to take action. One option is to start at the beginning and work systematically through the chapters. Another is to read through the book's chapter titles with your co-workers, skim the sections that seem most relevant or interesting to you, and find something you can do soon. Taking action is the best way to learn, and it gives you courage to keep taking action.

I hope, and pray, that because people like you are reading books like this, more people in suburbs and cities and countrysides will come to know Jesus Christ, and will introduce others to him. That is our call, whether we lead a parish, work in one, or just worship with others there: to go and make disciples of all nations.

Patrick Lencioni

Introduction

In my book *Divine Renovation*, I proposed a theology and model for how Catholic parishes could move from simply maintaining themselves to becoming missionary communities of disciples of Jesus Christ. That book is based on my own successes and failures as a parish priest, since the year 2000 when my bishop was crazy enough to put me in charge of a parish. Since 2010, this learning has intensified during my time as pastor of Saint Benedict Parish in Halifax, Nova Scotia.

Since *Divine Renovation* was published, our team has been grateful to receive many, many requests from wonderful priests and lay people around the world who wanted us to help them make their parishes missional. We were overwhelmed and saddened by the fact that we could help only a small fraction of them. And that's why this guidebook came about. Its purpose is simple: to provide pastors and their teams with the tools and information to ask the right questions and put the ideas from *Divine Renovation* into practice.

Now, I don't pretend to have all the answers here, or to have a single, prescriptive plan for transforming parishes. Every parish is different, and God has a unique plan for each one. However, I humbly submit that there are a few common denominators that must exist in almost any parish that is effectively bringing people to Jesus and his Church.

If you have already thumbed through these pages, you may be a bit intimidated. Don't be alarmed. The content of this book is meant to be worked through over the course of several years by a pastor, his leadership team and pastoral council.

My goal here is to keep this guidebook as user friendly, simple and understandable as it can possibly be. You will be my judge of how successful I was. My prayer is that the Holy Spirit will guide many, many parishes to use it in some way to more effectively go out into the world to make disciples of all nations.

God bless you all.
Fr. James Mallon

Do You Have to Read *Divine Renovation* to Use This Guidebook?

No, not necessarily, though it would certainly be helpful. Periodically, there are references to specific sections of *Divine Renovation*. The content and exercises in these pages presume that the reader has read those specific sections. For those who haven't read it yet, I present here a one-page summary of my experience at Saint Benedict Parish.

In 2010, I was named pastor of Saint Benedict Parish, which was the result of consolidating three previous parishes in Halifax. During my first few years at the helm, I made many decisions to help the parish become more effective in bringing people to Christ. Some of those ideas worked. Others didn't.

During that time, I met with great resistance from some staff members and parishioners, and was not able to convince them all to get on board and stay at the parish. I also overworked myself, leading to my battling lingering illnesses for long periods of time. After three years, by the grace of God, and with help from many incredible parishioners, my team and I were blessed to be able to lead the parish to a place we could not have imagined.

As of this writing, Saint Benedict has returned to the levels of attendance we saw in the first months of the new and curious church building being opened. Yes, you heard that right (but more on that later). More importantly, more than 40% of our parishioners are now involved in our discipleship process and disciple-making ministries. The numbers of parishioners in ministry has dramatically increased to 60%, and our weekend collection has doubled in six years. Of course, we aren't done, and we don't plan on taking credit for this or resting on our laurels. But we are confident that we have identified a number of important realities about what it takes to transform a parish from maintenance to mission, and what obstacles must be addressed and overcome in order to make that happen. We believe that these realities are transferable into your unique context.

Okay, enough about us. Let's start putting some of these ideas into practice in your parish.

The Pastor: It Starts with the Leader

The fact is, the leader of a parish is critical to its success. That sounds obvious, I realize. So let me put it another way. If the pastor of a parish is not prepared to lead the effort of transforming from maintenance to mission, then it simply isn't going to happen.

Fortunately, many pastors can do it. The vast majority of them love their vocation, even if they are tired or hurt. They want desperately to bring the people in their parish, whether they come to Mass on Sunday or not, to know and love Jesus through the Church he established more than two millennia ago.

But that isn't quite enough. While every pastor may have a different leadership capacity, every pastor has the capacity to be a better leader. A pastor is going to have to look at himself and be willing to address any shortcomings that could prevent his leadership from being successful. What might those shortcomings be?

For some, it might be the unwillingness to confront people and problems in the parish, and the desire to be liked by all staff members and parishioners all of the time. For others, it might be the belief that his schedule is simply too full to make changes, because those changes are only going to result in more work. For others still, it might be the fear of acknowledging weakness or admitting mistakes, which is often related to the difficulty of balancing the roles of being a parish's spiritual shepherd and its organizational leader.

Perhaps the most difficult challenge a pastor will face is the sense that he is doing all of this alone. We will deal with that in the following chapter on teamwork, but for now, let me make a specific recommendation. If you are not currently working with a leadership team (this is not your staff team or pastoral council), find a person in your parish to go through this guidebook with you. This could be a trusted senior staff member, or a parishioner who is a confidant, or a fellow priest. Find someone who will be your partner, your coach, because that will make it much more likely that the "aha" moments you have as you read this guidebook will become real changes.

So go ahead. Think of someone who can do this with you. Right now. We'll wait.

Okay, now write that person's name here:

_____

You might want to call them and have them join you before going further.

Personal Vision

 Go to divinerenovation.net. Under Media, go to Exploring themes and watch the second video, entitled "Leadership and Vision," until the 7:30 mark.

The pastor, Bill Hybels, has described "vision" as a picture of the future that produces passion in us. As you think about the future of your parish, what kind of parish would it have to be to make you passionate about it? What is the picture of the future that makes your heart beat faster and keeps you up at night, not with worry, but with excitement? I believe that answering this question is essential for every single leader, in ministry or otherwise. This is a question you must be able to answer before you can gather people around you to truly lead your parish.

If this picture of the future is difficult for you to enunciate, one strategy is to express the things in your parish right now that drive you crazy. The aspects of parish life that make you wince and say inside, or aloud, it can be better than this, will be the mirror image of what you are passionate about.

 At certain points along the way, I will be directing you to read specific portions of the book *Divine Renovation*. Watch for the book cover. Read about developing a vision for your parish on pages 244–253.

The pages that follow contain several exercises based on the pages mentioned above that will help you as a pastor find clarity about what you are passionate about and the direction in which you desire to lead your parish.

Prayer Support

If you've made it to this page, you may want to start thinking about recruiting special prayer support for what you are about to get into.

Spiritual warfare is real. The evil one does not desire to see the Church come to life. A maintenance parish or a parish in decline does not require his attention. However, as soon as you begin to shift your focus as a leader and engage your parish to begin this great journey, you will be on his radar.

In the next week, as you continue to work through these exercises, I strongly encourage you to connect with the leaders of the intercessory prayer groups in your parish. You don't need to give all the specifics, but ask them to commit to interceding for the renovation or renewal of the parish.

Take a moment. Think about the prayer ministry leaders and the prayer warriors in your parish and write their names below:

_____   _____

_____   _____

_____   _____

What is Your Discontent?

Within your sphere of influence, what are the things about your ministry that drive you crazy? What is it that makes you think, "It doesn't have to be this way; it can be better than this!" Take some time to reflect on this prayerfully and write these things below.

What Does Your Parish Look Like in Ten Years?

What is your dream for your parish? If anything were possible, what would it look and feel like? Describe it. Don't write down a plan, but your dream. Use as much space as you like: don't be limited to this page.

My personal purpose statement:

Create a one-sentence personal purpose statement that summarizes your ministry and calling at this time in your life.

 @SaintBP

Throughout the guidebook I will be giving examples of what we do at Saint Benedict Parish on a particular topic.

Regarding personal purpose statements for ministry, we ask all our staff to develop one-sentence job descriptions. While this can be challenging and frustrating, it is also a great source of clarity and helps each member be mindful of their main focus.

Charisms Reflection

As mentioned on pages 250–251 of *Divine Renovation*, charisms – the God-given passions and gifts we have received – will play a great role in shaping our vision and sense of purpose. This is okay. The key is to be aware of it.

Most people are strong in two or three of the charisms mentioned in Paul's Letter to the Ephesians (4:11). Take a few moments to reflect on this passage of Scripture, then choose and rank your top three charisms.

Now go back and reread your vision statement (see page 14) and your purpose statement (see page 15) and reflect on how your charisms have shaped what you have written.

CHARISM	DESIRE	RANK THREE
Apostle	to go outside the Church	
Prophet	to speak out, to be annoying	
Evangelist	to bring people to Jesus	
Pastor	to care for people within the Church	
Teacher	to teach/doctrine/knowledge	

2

The Team: The Pastor Can't Do It Alone

That word – team – gets used so often that it has lost much of its meaning. A team is not just a group of people who happen to work together. In a parish, a leadership team is not just the staff members who happen to work in the office. And it's certainly not a parish council or finance council.

A parish leadership team is a group of people – most likely between four and six members – who share responsibility for the success of the parish with the pastor. Of course, they understand and honour the authority of the pastor, but they take responsibility for helping him do what is needed to make the parish amazing.

Who is on the leadership team? That is going to depend on the size, nature and makeup of the parish, of course. But, generally, it will include key senior staff members who oversee major areas of responsibility. Maybe religious education or operations or liturgies, or whatever you call those things in your parish. And in many cases, an associate priest may be included. Perhaps the first member of your leadership team is reading this chapter along with you right now, as the person you identified at the beginning of Chapter 1.

But the members of the leadership team will not be chosen solely based on their areas of responsibility. They will also be mature, trustworthy, influential and capable of having strategic conversations. And they will see the parish as a whole, not merely in terms of their department or ministry. They will be willing to jump into critical topics or areas in the parish that need addressing, and often without much notice.

Do you have to disband your current staff team, or uninvite people from it, in order to create a leadership team? No. It is about creating a brand new team and explaining its purpose clearly to anyone concerned. What about the parish council or finance council? Aren't they going to be upset if they aren't part of the leadership team? Not if the purpose of the new team is made clear.

Now, there is no guarantee that a staff member or two, or a council member or two, won't resist or rebel, even if the pastor has adequately and gracefully explained the reason for the new leadership team. If that's the case, then there is good reason to help those people find their way to another parish. While building a team does not necessarily require losing current staff members or parishioners, it certainly requires the willingness to do so. There is nothing unkind about that. Really.

Go to divinerenovation.net. Under Media, go to Exploring themes and watch the third video, entitled "Forming a Leadership Team."

Who should be on my leadership team?

Many factors go into building a successful leadership team. At Saint Benedict Parish, we stress four non-negotiables:

1) Unanimity of vision
2) Balance of strengths
3) Healthy conflict and trust
4) Vulnerability

@SaintBP

The four non-negotiables of a leadership team:

1) Unanimity of vision
2) Balance of strengths
3) Healthy conflict and trust
4) Vulnerability

Let's take a closer look at each of these.

1) Unanimity of vision

Vision is essentially about where the parish is heading. Imagine four people in a canoe in the middle of a lake. Each person is paddling frantically towards a different shore. You know what is going to happen: nothing – or at best, they will go round and round in circles, getting exhausted and going nowhere.

Leadership teams are teams where members should openly disagree about the best way to move towards fulfilling the vision, but the very basis of this rich disagreement is a fundamental commitment to the one vision. If there are two visions, there will be di-vision. Division at the core of the parish leadership will produce division throughout the entire parish.

Let's begin with helping you identify the staff members and key parishioners who share your passion for that distant shore. They will be the pool from which you will build your leadership team.

Take some time to write the names of the most influential people in your parish in the boxes on the next page. These can be all or some of your staff, or key parishioners, ministry leads or pastoral council members. Next, identify the groups of parishioners they have influence over. For instance, the Grand Knight of the Knights of Columbus has influence over all the other Knights. If he can be won over to your vision, he will become a vision carrier to the whole group.

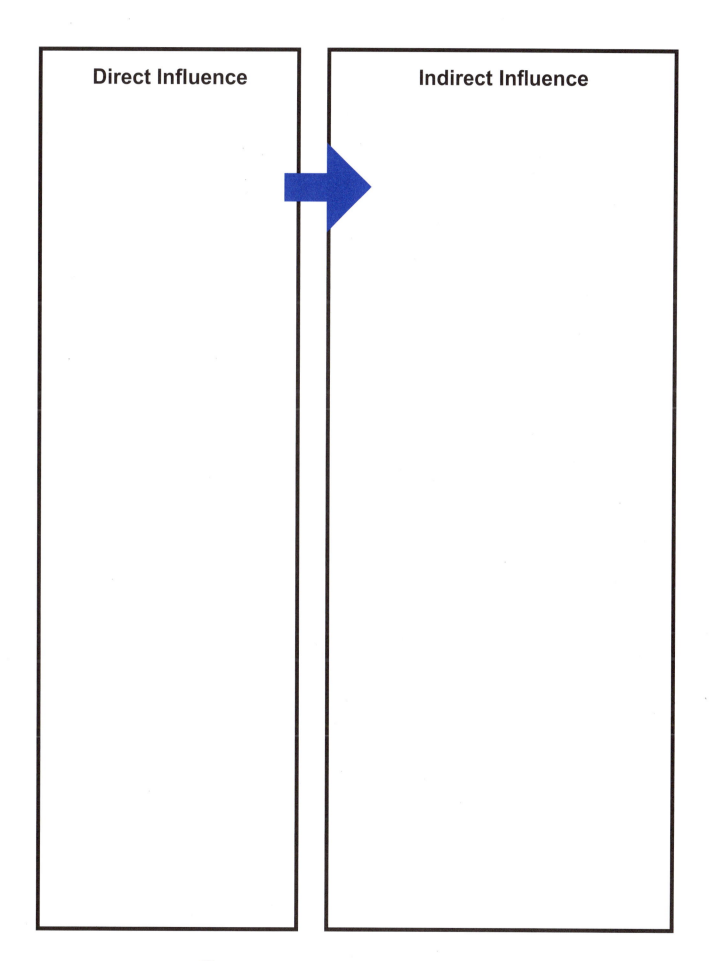

Take some time in the next few weeks to invest in your key staff and parishioners. Share your dream for your parish with them. Listen to theirs. Listen carefully to what they are passionate about. Don't presume that because you share a love and commitment to your parish that you have the same vision.

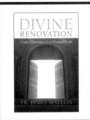 Read "Communicating the Vision" on pages 253–258.

For your leadership team, you are looking for three to five people to join you. As you share your heart with your key influential staff and parishioners, identify below those who are strong candidates for your leadership team. Remember, at this point you want to focus on common vision. A secondary goal is to identify the most influential members of your staff or parish with whom you share vision.

The chart below depicts four possibilities:

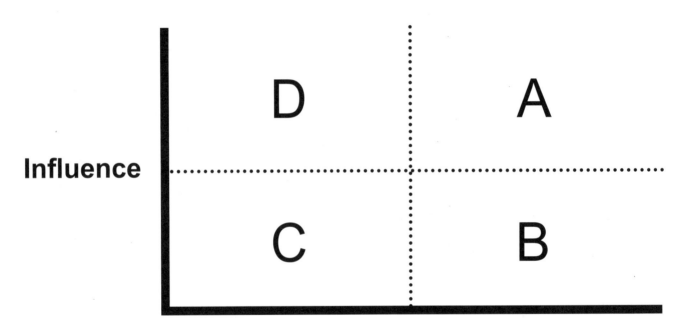

Option D represents high influence and low common vision.
Option C represents low influence and low common vision.
Option B represents low influence and high common vision.
Option A represents high influence and high common vision.

Obviously, the goal is to have as many "A" parishioners and staff as possible on your leadership team.

Prefer a "B" member over a "D" member. A person with strong influence who does not share the vision will frustrate and bring division to your team.

Take some time to write on the next page the names of the top contenders for your leadership team and the category in which they fit.

Name	Fit (A,B,C or D)	Name	Fit (A,B,C or D)

Now let's look at the second non-negotiable for your leadership team.

The principles that I am basing this strategy on are taken from *The Five Dysfunctions of a Team*, by Patrick Lencioni. I cannot recommend this book highly enough. It will be a huge help to you as you build a leadership team. What you will find on the following pages is strongly influenced by Pat's thoughts.

2) Balance of strengths

There is no such thing as a balanced person! We are all a little odd (some of us more than others). There is, however, a balanced team. As a pastor, you have specific strengths, but also specific weaknesses. Lean into your strengths, and instead of trying to bolster your weaknesses, bring a team around you that balances you. This is what a leadership team is meant to do.

Read about strengths-based ministry on pages 164–168 and balanced teams on pages 241–242.

Another way to think about it is that we all have blind spots. Imagine a leadership team of five people, all with the exact same strengths and the exact same blind spots. Talk about the blind leading the blind!

Your team, however, is *your* team. They must be built around your specific strengths. This means that the members must be strong where you are weak. The first step, then, is for you to undertake an evaluation of your own particular talents or strengths before you identify those of others. Don't do this alone, and use a tool.

 @SaintBP

At Saint Benedict Parish we have relied heavily on the Clifton Strengths Finder from Gallup. This is easy to access and can be done online at gallupstrengthscenter.com. We have also used the Birkman Method of evaluation (birkman.com).

There are many ways to do this. At Saint Benedict Parish we have relied heavily on the Clifton Strengths Finder from Gallup. This is easy to access and can be done on-line at gallupstrengthscenter.com. We have also used the Birkman Method of evaluation (birkman.com). Myers Briggs, Tracom's Social Style Model, or the DISC Method can also be used. What matters is that you choose a tool and work with it.

At this point we are evaluating natural talents. These are to be distinguished from spiritual gifts. Tools by which we identify spiritual gifts can be tremendously helpful for equipping parishioners to do ministry. They focus on *what* a person is called to do by God. Tools measuring natural ability will identify *how* a person will do what they are called to do.

As mentioned in *Divine Renovation*, the Clifton Strengths Finder categorizes its 34 themes of talent into four general categories: Executing, Influencing, Relationship Building and Strategic Thinking.

I highly recommend that you take the time to do the Clifton Strengths Finder online assessment to identify your top five themes. It won't take you long. After you have completed your online testing at the Gallup Strengths Center, use the chart on the next page to map out your top five themes. Write your name in each applicable box.

When you have completed this task, ask those whom you identified at the end of the last exercise to identify their top themes of talent using the same Gallup tools. Begin to map the names on the chart.

Executing		Influencing		Relationship Building		Strategic Thinking	
Catch an idea and make things happen. Work tirelessly to get it done.		*Help team reach a broader audience. Sell ideas in and out of organization. Speak up and take charge.*		*Glue that holds team together. Ability to create groups and organizations greater than the sum of their parts.*		*Focused on what could be. They are constantly absorbing and analyzing info and helping the team make better decisions.*	
ACHIEVER		ACTIVATOR		ADAPTABILITY		ANALYTICAL	
ARRANGER		COMMAND		CONNECTEDNESS		CONTEXT	
BELIEF		COMMUNICATION		DEVELOPER		FUTURISTIC	
CONSISTENCY		COMPETITION		EMPATHY		IDEATION	
DELIBERATIVE		MAXIMIZER		HARMONY		INPUT	
DISCIPLINE		SELF-ASSURANCE		INCLUDER		INTELLECTION	
FOCUS		SIGNIFICANCE		INDIVIDUALIZATION		LEARNER	
RESPONSIBILITY		WOO		POSITIVITY		STRATEGIC	
RESTORATIVE				RELATOR			

2 The Team: The Pastor Can't Do It Alone

Questions for reflection

1) In which of the four categories are you strongest? Where are you weakest?

2) Can any immediately identifiable candidates compensate for your weaknesses?

3) Is any category not adequately covered? Do you need to expand your search?

Keep all the names on your chart. You will be going back to these.

Below is another tool developed by Tracom Group to help you build a balanced team. It provides a framework for self-analysis of your own work style. You may wish to use this tool to map your social style if you do not use the Clifton Strengths Finder. Ask for feedback from those you work with about this, as they may know more about how you work than you do.

Task

Analytical	Driver
Amiable	Expressive

Ask (left) *Tell* (right)

People

This tool is fairly intuitive. Make an attempt to map your social style simply by asking yourself, "Am I more of a people person or a task person?" And "When I work with others, do I tend to ask or tell?"

Now ask at least three of the people you work with what they think about your work style and adjust as necessary.

These categories can be further subdivided, as seen below. Where do you fit? Once again, seek feedback from members in your group.

Task

Analytical	Driver	Analytical	Driver
Analytical		**Driver**	
Amiable	Expressive	Amiable	Expressive
Analytical	Driver	Analytical	Driver
Amiable		**Expressive**	
Amiable	Expressive	Amiable	Expressive

Ask ... ***Tell***

People

On the next page, map the social styles of the candidates for your leadership team. Do this exercise together. Don't be too serious – have a few laughs.

Map the work styles of your team members

Task

	Analytical	Driver		Analytical	Driver
Ask	**Analytical**			**Driver**		**Tell**
	Amiable	Expressive		Amiable	Expressive
	Analytical	Driver		Analytical	Driver
	Amiable			**Expressive**	
	Amiable	Expressive		Amiable	Expressive

People

Questions for reflection

1) In which of the four categories are you strongest? Where are you weakest?

2) Can any immediately identifiable candidates compensate for your weaknesses?

3) Is any category not adequately covered? Do you need to expand your search?

Keep all the names on your chart. You will be going back to these again.

Four Styles

Analytical: "Look before you leap"

plans researches, collects data, analyzes, exact, detail-oriented, perfectionist, cautious, skeptical, prepared, thorough

Amiable: "Let's work together"

wants to get along, people-oriented, dislikes conflict, supportive, helpful, builds relationships, giving, honest, picks up subtleties

Driver: "Get it done"

direct, dutiful, practical, decisive, fast-paced, lead not follow, results, on time, on task

Expressive: "Trust me"

energetic, inspiring, fast, flamboyant, playful, creative, rapid reactor, flexible, non-linear, tests limits

---

Remember, the goal of this exercise is to identify potential team members who compensate for your weaknesses and blind spots. No matter what tool you use, giftedness, talents or styles are generally grouped into four quadrants. If your leadership team is to have four to six members, the goal is to have all four quadrants covered.

Let's move now to the third non-negotiable of a leadership team.

3) Healthy conflict and trust

As mentioned in the first section, on vision, the primary key to a successful leadership team is unanimity of vision. A shared passion for the desired future of your parish is the foundation for engaging in healthy conflict over strategy and tactics. Not only is this open disagreement tolerated, it is desired. This, however, is easier said than done.

For healthy conflict to exist, there must be trust. Only trust allows team members to express different opinions, to disagree with the pastor, and do so safely. Many leaders lack self-awareness in this regard. They think they provide a safe place for constructive disagreement, but they can fool themselves. This can happen in several ways:

1) There is no balance in the team. Members share the same blind spots, which limits healthy conflict.
2) The pastor gathers around himself a group of "YES" people who would never dare to disagree with him, even though they see what he does not: "Yes, Father, no Father, three bags full, Father…"
3) The pastor has a balanced team of capable people, but members do not feel safe. Disagreement with the pastor can have serious consequences after the meeting. As a result, people do not say what they really think: they see the train wreck coming and are ready with an "I told you so" to one another when the wreck takes place.
4) The pastor has a balanced team of capable people, but he will silence any disagreement with a glance or his body language, even without realizing he is doing this. The results are the same.

Patrick Lencioni says that "conflict without trust is politics." We all know that effective teamwork is too often limited by interpersonal politics within church circles.

What is the answer to this?
1) As the leader, be self-aware.
2) Gather team members who are free to challenge the pastor and speak their minds.
3) Work constantly at establishing a culture of trust and love within your leadership team.

Think of the teams you work with the most. In all likelihood, these will be your staff team and your pastoral council. Take some time to reflect on your experience of these teams and assess the health of your teams by doing the exercise on the next page.

Write your scores down on the page beside the statement. When you are finished, go to the next page and collate your results.

When you are finished, ask the members of your various teams to complete the exercise. Obviously, many of these team members will be on the short list for your leadership team.

Compare results and take time to discuss and truly listen to those who support you in your ministry. You might be surprised by what you hear.

Assess the health of your team

3=Usually   2=Sometimes   1=Rarely

1. Team members are passionate and unguarded in their discussion of issues.

2. Team members quickly and genuinely apologize to one another when they say or do something inappropriate or possibly damaging to the team.

3. Team members openly admit their weaknesses and mistakes.

4. Team meetings are compelling and not boring.

5. During team meetings, the most important and most difficult issues are put on the table to be resolved.

6. Team members know about one another's personal lives and are comfortable discussing them.

Adapted from *The Five Dysfunctions of a Team* by Patrick Lencioni.

Team Assessment Scoring

Behaviour 1: Building Trust	Behaviour 2: Mastering Conflict
Statement 2 ____ Statement 3 ____ Statement 6 ____	Statement 1 ____ Statement 4 ____ Statement 5 ____
Total:	**Total:**

A score of 8 or 9 is a probable indication that the Behaviour is not a problem for your team.
A score of 6 or 7 indicates that the Behaviour could be a problem.
A score of 3 to 5 is an indication that the Behaviour needs to be addressed.

Adapted from *The Five Dysfunctions of a Team* by Patrick Lencioni.

Assess the health of your team

3=Usually   2=Sometimes   1=Rarely

1. Team members are passionate and unguarded in their discussion of issues.

2. Team members quickly and genuinely apologize to one another when they say or do something inappropriate or possibly damaging to the team.

3. Team members openly admit their weaknesses and mistakes.

4. Team meetings are compelling and not boring.

5. During team meetings, the most important and most difficult issues are put on the table to be resolved.

6. Team members know about one another's personal lives and are comfortable discussing them.

Adapted from *The Five Dysfunctions of a Team* by Patrick Lencioni.

Team Assessment Scoring

Behaviour 1: Building Trust	Behaviour 2: Mastering Conflict
Statement 2 ____ Statement 3 ____ Statement 6 ____	Statement 1 ____ Statement 4 ____ Statement 5 ____
Total:	**Total:**

A score of 8 or 9 is a probable indication that the Behaviour is not a problem for your team.
A score of 6 or 7 indicates that the Behaviour could be a problem.
A score of 3 to 5 is an indication that the Behaviour needs to be addressed.

Adapted from *The Five Dysfunctions of a Team* by Patrick Lencioni.

Questions for reflection

1) Was there a significant difference between your assessment of team behaviours and that of the members of your various teams?

2) What did you hear from your team members about how you can grow in leading a team that can engage in healthy conflict?

3) What did you hear from your team members about how there can be greater trust?

4) Who were the team members most capable of speaking on these issues?

5) Who were the members who did not contribute to the discussion?

It should be noted that Patrick Lencioni names another three behaviours that contribute to a strong leadership team: achieving commitment, embracing accountability, and focusing on results. More details can be found in his book *The Five Dysfunctions of a Team*.

Let's now look at the fourth non-negotiable of a leadership team.

4) Vulnerability

Vulnerability is about being real. The truth is that if we set out on the journey from maintenance to mission, if it actually works, we will soon find ourselves in unfamiliar territory. Managing a parish in maintenance mode will not take us to a new place; therefore, there is a good chance that as leaders we will be fairly competent in our ministries. When a parish begins to move, however, the pastor will eventually find himself in a place where certainty about what exactly to do next will quickly disappear. The first and most necessary vulnerability, therefore, is that of the pastor who needs to say to his team, "I need you. I no longer know what to do."

Read about vulnerability and leadership on pages 240–244.

Going on this great adventure of leading your parish from maintenance to mission will involve great risk, great rewards and great fun. Along the way, there will be sparks. Why? Because you have gathered a group of passionate, capable people in an environment that seeks to engage in healthy conflict. How do we stop sparks from causing the wrong kind of fire? By creating a culture of vulnerability and caring at the heart of our leadership team. It is about being real: the pastor with his team and team members with one another.

Team members – no matter how committed to the vision and how capable of engaging in conversation they are – who hold their cards close to their chests and cannot be real with the other members will sink a leadership team.

So far you have identified your key people and discerned their alignment with your vision. You have mapped out the potential members who would be part of a balanced team and you have evaluated your own and your future team members' ability to engage in healthy conflict. Vulnerability is the final piece of the puzzle.

I would like to propose two team exercises to help you be vulnerable with one another and help you discern who would best serve on your leadership team. Chances are that you already have a good sense of who really struggles with being vulnerable, but these exercises may be useful.

Sharing Exercise

This one is simple. At the beginning of your next staff or pastoral council meeting, take a moment to go around your team and have everyone share a high and a low from the last month. It can be from their ministry or personal life. Pay attention to see who plays it really safe and describes their high and low without being vulnerable in any way (it can be done).

Prayer Exercise

This is an exercise I have used over the last number of years when speaking with groups of clergy. It really calls people to step outside the box and can be slightly uncomfortable. For that reason I introduce the main exercise through a series of warm-up exercises.

Ask your team to form groups of three or four. Try to have even numbers in each group. The groups can be seated or standing together. One person will have to be a time keeper and keep the exercise moving.

1) First exercise: *Thanksgiving*

    Each person takes a turn praying out loud in the hearing of the others. They pray a 30-second prayer of thanksgiving to God, such as, "Lord, I thank you for..." while others listen. After 30 seconds, the time keeper calls time and invites the second person to begin.

2) Second exercise: *Petition*

    Each person takes a turn praying out loud in the hearing of the others so the others can hear. They pray a 1-minute prayer of petition to God, such as, "Lord, I ask you…" while others listen. After 1 minute, the time keeper calls time and invites the second person to begin.

3) Third exercise: *Receiving Prayer*

Each person expresses to the others something they would like to receive prayer for. After asking permission, the other members take turns praying out loud over that person as they place a hand on the shoulder or the head of the one receiving the prayer. A total of 3 minutes is set for each person to receive prayer from the other group members. After 3 minutes, the time keeper calls time and invites the second person to begin.

When this exercise has concluded, bring the group back together and take some time to discuss the following questions:

1) What was easy?

2) What was difficult?

3) What surprised you?

Take note of who does or does not share and who was willing to enter into this exercise, in spite of it being outside of their comfort zone.

Conclusion

As mentioned at the beginning of this chapter, building a leadership team is one of the most crucial things you can do for the journey that lies ahead. These exercises around the four non-negotiables, plus what you already know, will give you all you need to discern the members of your team from among your key staff and parishioners. There is no algorithm for this. Who are the most aligned to your vision? Who are the most able to engage in healthy conflict? Who are capable of vulnerability? From among these, choose those who will bring balance to your team.

Remember: you only need to choose three to five. Write their names here:

@SaintBP

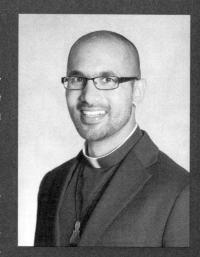

The following is one of a series of weekly reflections by Fr. Simon Lobo, CC, the associate pastor of Saint Benedict Parish (SBP), who is currently on a three-year learning internship.

"Learning to Say No," February 26, 2016

Nerf guns have become a necessity at our SLT (Senior Leadership Team) meetings, and they reveal something of our culture. Our meetings are both intense and fun! Patrick Lencioni made the observation that most people are happy to sit through a two-hour movie which has little or no bearing on their lives. On the flip side, people are bored out of their minds in an equally long meeting. In the former we do not actively participate. If the latter is boring, it is because we do not actively participate – and we fail to speak about the things that matter. There is a high level of trust and healthy conflict among our SLT, which allows for interesting and "dangerous" meetings.

Initially, I found these meetings difficult, but I have come to see their value. The other day FJM (Fr. James Mallon) reminded us of one of the first SLT meetings when I was present. The discussion got heated, and so he looked over at me to make sure I was still okay. I guess my complexion must have been slightly paler than normal. Over time I have been able to bring more things to the table and have gotten better at expressing my opinions.

Many months ago I wrote about saying NO to a parishioner who had a request that I – as priest – did not need to be directly involved with. A few weeks ago I found myself in a similar, but different, scenario when someone from outside the parish approached me. This married layman is about my age and zealous for the Kingdom, and he has developed a new apostolate focused on evangelization. I love what they are doing! In fact, I have had a few opportunities in the past to do some ministry alongside them and it has always been an easy fit, loads of fun, and very fruitful. So you can imagine my excitement when he proposed a kind of a partnership with SBP. Still, from the beginning there was a part of me that was hesitant. We have already developed a clear and involved model, and this would mean embracing a second ministry model (which also happens to be well thought-out and mission-oriented).

When the discussion came up at SLT, everyone else quickly confirmed my hunch. We all love their organization and feel united by the same yearning to bring people to Jesus in the power of the Holy Spirit. However, it would not make sense to try to mesh the two strategies. We simply need to stick to our SBP GAME PLAN. It is interesting to note that different people process information and arrive at decisions at various speeds. FJM and Ron are probably the fastest in our group. Kate, who always has profound insights, usually needs a lot more time. I would suggest that Rob and I are somewhere in the middle. At any rate, the others could see that I was still wrestling with having to say NO to this brother in the vineyard. They did not leave me but insisted that I try to share my difficulties. In the end it was just a question of me needing time to process the decision. Intellectually, I knew it was the correct way to go, but I still needed to struggle with it emotionally.

What do I want you to know?

After the fact, FJM jokingly said, "Now you know how I feel." He is constantly being approached by great people, with incredible ministries, who have a desire to partner. I was amazed to hear some of the household names (in the Catholic world) that he has had to turn down, not the least of which would be *EWTN*.

After our conversation, FJM tweeted the following: "Saying NO to bad ideas is easy. Saying NO to good ideas is difficult, but often necessary if a church is going to be intentional and focused."

What do I want you to do?

I may sound like a broken record, but you need to clarify the vision. What is the future picture of your parish that excites you? Then you need to formulate a strategy to start moving people in that direction. When those things become more obvious, you can courageously say NO to all the other good ideas that do not align themselves with the vision and strategy of your particular parish.

Second, leaders need to establish teams around themselves who understand the vision and strategy and who can keep them accountable. FJM admits that left to his own devices – even when he has intellectual clarity about saying NO – his tendency is to give in and say YES. Do you have a culture where the people around the table feel comfortable keeping the leader focused? If not, think about ways to help the team members to feel safe enough to vocalize their opinions.

The Prep: Being Strategic about Being Strategic

Congratulations on arriving at Chapter 3. I hope you are reading this chapter not just with one other person now, but with your newly formed leadership team (unless you already had one). As pastor, you are no longer alone. It is not simply about leading a team but leading *out of* a team. They are not the same thing. As you enter into the challenge of leading renewal, based on the principles we outlined in the last chapter, you will know what I mean. The good news is that you are not alone on this journey.

So what do we do now? Make a plan? Not yet. Too often, churches succumb to the temptation of making a plan before they have established clarity around other critical factors.

George Harrison, in his song "Any Road," said, "If you don't know where you are going, any road will get you there." When setting out on a journey, the first question we ask is "Where are we going?" That is a question about Vision. Knowing where you want to go is a start, but it's still not enough to make a plan.

I often think of my experience going shopping. I hate shopping. I go to malls once every two years, usually when I need new shoes. I like to get in and get out. The first thing I do is find one of those big maps that shows where all the stores are. I know where I want to go, so I look for the shoe store on the map. This is like vision. I know my desired destination, but I still do not have enough information to make a plan for how to get my new shoes.

What do I do next? What do I look for? You know the answer!

I look for the big YOU ARE HERE dot. I need to know where I currently am before I can make a plan.

Okay, so we are ready to make that plan now, right? Not quite.

Think about the shopping mall. I know where the shoe store is on the map and I know where I am on the map, but as I look around me, I realize that I have not established which way is which. I need to match what I see on the map with what I see in front of my eyes. I need a compass. When it comes to your parish, you also need a compass. Clarity of purpose serves as this compass.

Now you are ready to make a plan – or, in other words, develop a strategy. You know where you want to go, you know what your starting point is and you have a compass.

Finding clarity on these points is essential, but before we delve into these matters, I wish to take some time with you and your team to ensure that you are set up for success. I call this being strategic about being strategic.

Being Strategic About Being Strategic

 Read about being strategic about being strategic on pages 258–266.

 Read about the challenge of living out a different model of priestly ministry on pages 170–173, in the section entitled "Clerical Culture," and about the essentials of priestly ministry on pages 75–76, in the section entitled "Sorting Through the Confusion."

As I said in *Divine Renovation*, at Saint Benedict Parish I eventually realized that the leadership structures that were in place in my parish, as well as the expectations around how I would minister as a priest, were obstacles to beginning to operate strategically as a parish. To be honest, some of my team members saw it long before I did. There was much frustration and pain before I was able to see it. Perhaps the exercises in the following pages can save your team some time, as well as spare you some frustration and pain.

Let's take a look at these two areas of parish life, beginning with the ministry expectations of the pastor.

The Pastor Himself

At this point in the guidebook, you have already invested considerable time and energy in getting to this chapter. The problem is that you have been investing this time and energy in addition to doing all the other things expected of you as pastor, as well as responding to the unscheduled and short-notice demands of ministry. We all know, all too well, that in parishes, the most important things are often left untended because of the most urgent things. Rarely do they coincide.

The truth is that to lead your parish from maintenance to mission, you will need to adjust how you minister and how you lead in your parish. You will need the support of your leadership team not just to remind parishioners about why things are changing, but to remind *you* about why things are changing, to hold you accountable to these changes and to give you permission to stay the course.

The Second Vatican Council reminded bishops and priests, in many places, that their ministry was to embody the threefold ministry of Jesus, who was Prophet, Priest and King. The prophetic ministry is related to the preaching of the Word of God, the priestly ministry with the celebration of the sacraments, especially the Eucharist, and the kingly ministry has to do with leading God's people.

Due to the clerical culture that is present in so many of our parishes, there is an expectation that the priest must be involved in every ministry so it may have legitimacy. He is expected to be available to any and all people to be their personal chaplain. This means very little time is left for the essentials of priesthood.

As a result, time for preaching is shortchanged, and very little time is left for any exercise of leadership. What is being proposed in this book is going to make new demands on the time of the pastor so he can exercise leadership. This will mean letting go of some of the non-essentials.

In my work with priests over the years, when I ask them about the percentage of time they spend fulfilling the essential tasks of the priesthood (preaching, celebrating sacraments and leading) as opposed to all the other demands of ministry, their answers are shocking. Many will say that as little as 20% to 40% of their time goes into these essential tasks. If they were to map out how they spend their time, it may look like this:

Pastor's Weekly Ministry Assessment

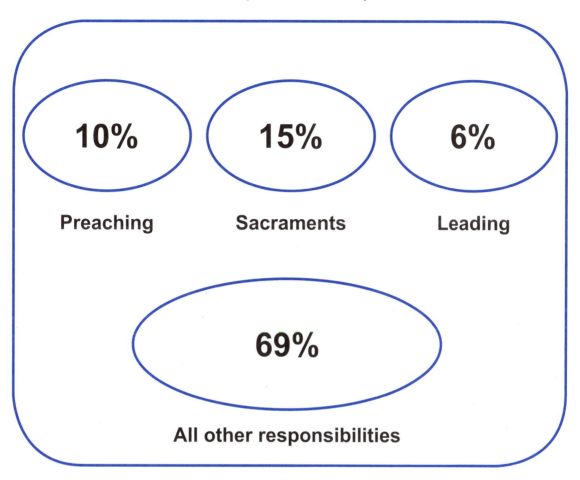

The chart above presumes that we have a priest who is working about 60 to 70 hours a week and is also enriching his life with prayer, exercise and relational support on top of these working hours.

Pastor's Weekly Ministry Assessment

Work together as a team and identify the breakdown of how the pastor spends his time in ministry. Remember that managing things is not leadership.

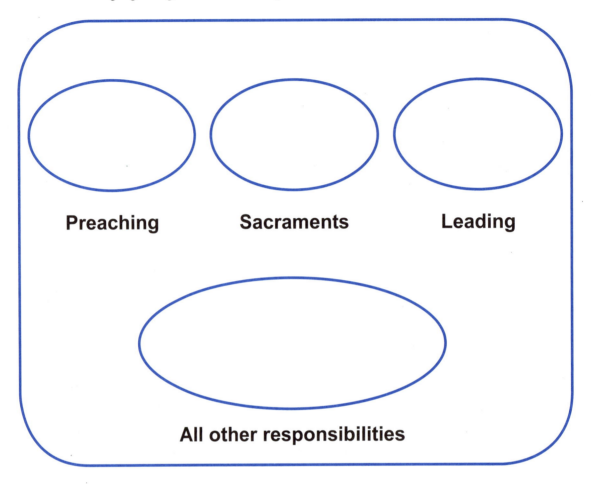

Let's take some time to unpack what you have discovered.

Are you as a team surprised by what you see? Discuss this together.

Now I'd like to ask you this: What would your parish look like if 80% of the pastor's time could be put into ministry essential to the priesthood? It is possible to get to that, and it will make a huge difference in your parish.

Let's begin by mapping out the tasks and responsibilities that compose the non-essential ministry, and the hours they involve.

TASKS	HOURS

The goal in the next year or two should be for the priest to divest himself of most of these non-essential ministries so he can reach the 80% mark. This is easier said than done, as we have to change not just our own attitudes and expectations but those of the people around us. Unless the pastor does this, he will never be free to lead his parish from maintenance to mission, and his parishioners will be limited in their maturity.

I call it the "push out factor." The more you can push out these ministries that have been associated with the role of the priest – but are not essential to it – the more free you will be to invest in the essentials, and the more responsibility your parishioners will take on. Growth will take place for both reasons.

This is about pushing out, not about pushing away. You cannot divest yourself of these ministries, roles and tasks until you have called and equipped others to take them on. This will take time, so be patient.

Take some time below to group the demands of non-essential ministry into categories. In my own experience as a priest, they could be something like this:

1) Administrative duties: everything associated with buildings, finances, procedures, and policy.
2) Non-sacramental pastoral care: these can include hospital visits and visiting the sick in their homes.
3) Funeral ministry: all the planning and preparation for funerals to the funeral liturgy itself.
4) One on one: this can include pastoral counselling, spiritual direction and generally being available for anyone who wants to come in and chat.
5) Weddings: interviews, marriage preparation, arguing with mothers-in-law and bridezillas, rehearsals and liturgies.
6) Meetings: the wrong type of meeting: the meetings you do not need to be at.

Perhaps you can think of a few more categories. The truth is that most priests spend most of their time in these categories of non-essential ministry. Unless you are ministering in a parish of less than 200 people, this is hugely counter-productive.

Take some time on the next page to put your non-essential ministry hours into categories and add up the total time involved in each. When you have done this, take a moment to rank each category in terms of priority for pushing out.

Category	Time	Rank

In many larger parishes, pushing out will involve hiring additional staff, but many of the pastor's responsibilities can be taken on by current staff or delegated to competent lay people in the parish. I am using the term *responsibilities* intentionally. We cannot simply push out tasks. Tasks without responsibility will always be handed back to you.

@SaintBP

My first priority when I began my ministry at Saint Benedict Parish was to confirm a staffing position called Director of Operations. This position was responsible for all aspects of parish administration and oversaw all admin staff and operational ministries. When I speak with priests I am often shocked at how much of their time and energy goes into these kind of tasks and I am grateful that I have been able to have such amazing staff who can free me from those responsibilities.

The second task was to form and train teams of parishioners who would visit the sick in the hospital and at home. The Sacrament of the Sick is offered once a month at a weekday Mass and we will go to homes to anoint parishioners if they are unable to come to us. Outside of this, I am generally not available for this kind of ministry.

When I arrived at Saint Benedict Parish I was blessed to inherit a ministry established by the previous pastor. The Funeral Team members were the first responders for funerals. They met with the families, prepared the liturgy, and gave me the information I would need to celebrate the funeral Mass and preach. Deacons do the vigil prayers and the grave site prayers, and, if they are not available, members of the Funeral Team do this. In a parish that has 50 to 60 funerals a year, this minimizes the impact of short-notice funerals.

Regarding one-on-one ministry, I knew in my head that I could fill up my entire schedule with people who wanted to see me, and for many years I did. Two things happened: I never got to meet with the people I needed to meet with, and I used up all my available time. I had virtually no time to answer emails, prepare homilies, talks and presentations, never mind time to even think, plan and lead. I became exhausted and trapped. I would block off time for all of these tasks and would end up sacrificing these time blocks because I felt really bad about having to tell someone I couldn't see them for three weeks. After struggling with this for years, I realized that I literally could not help myself. I needed someone to protect me from myself and my own inability to say no. I now have a personal assistant who controls every aspect of my schedule. She protects the margin in my schedule that I need to prepare, to think, to live, breathe, pray, exercise and to lead. The best thing is that I never have to say no to anyone. I have four half-hour blocks each week to meet with people who want to see me. My assistant gently and kindly does the best she can.

Finally, meetings! The question is not about whether or not you will be in meetings, but about which meetings you are in. In truth, as you lean more into the task of leading, your time in meetings will radically increase, but they will be the right type of meetings.

> Currently at Saint Benedict Parish we have about 70 ministries, a plethora of mid-size and small groups, Alpha etc. We have thousands of events of some kind each year. What meetings do I go to? A weekly Senior Leadership Team (SLT) meeting, weekly clergy team meeting, ad hoc strategic meetings every few months, monthly All Staff meeting, bi-monthly Pastoral Council, monthly Finance Committee and one-on-one meetings with my key staff members (about 25% of my staff). Oversight of ministry leaders is the responsibility of various staff, and most of my staff report directly to three other staff members who report to me.
>
> About weddings, presently 95% of all the work around marriage and weddings is done by deacons and lay people.
>
> In truth, right now at Saint Benedict Parish, 99% of the ministry that takes place is not done by me. What do I do? I preach the Word of God, I celebrate the sacraments, I lead and I am now at the point where I am able to commit 80% of my time and energy to these tasks.

I realize that some people may be alarmed by the model of ministry I am proposing above. However, unless you are in a very small parish, you will likely have to adjust how you exercise your priesthood. If you are in a parish that has a weekend attendance greater than 1,000 people, you will have to change if you wish to actually lead it on the path to mission.

Three primary things hinder us from moving towards this model:

1. Our own neediness: my own need to be needed. This is often hidden in the aspects of ministry we "love" to do.
2. My own expectations: my self-understanding of what it means to be a "good priest."
3. The expectations of others: spoken or unspoken, often shaped in a bygone era. New layers of expectation have been added, but none have been taken away.

Questions for reflection and discussion with your leadership team

1. What needs of yours are being met by your involvement in non-essential ministry?
2. How do you experience a need to be needed?
3. What aspects of non-essential ministry do you find especially life-giving? These will generally be reflective of your core charisms that you identified in Chapter 1.
4. What maximum amount of time can you give to these "life-giving" ministries?
5. As you consider your list of non-essential tasks and responsibilities, which ones have you taken on due to your own self-expectations?
6. Your parishioners have expectations of you and your ministry. Which expectations do you *feel* are reasonable and which are unreasonable? Which ones do you *think* are reasonable and which are unreasonable?

7. How does guilt operate in your ministry life? When are you inclined to feel like a "bad priest"?

8. How can your leadership team hold you accountable for becoming more focused on the essentials of priestly ministry?

Before we leave the topic of the pastor's ministry, let me encourage you to take this very seriously. As a parish moves from maintenance to mission, it will begin to wake up, come to life and grow. If a pastor is not prepared to adapt his model of leadership and ministry, he will be crushed and will never see it through.

The choice is simple: 1) cling to an outdated, clerically centred model of ministry, have limited impact and burn out, or 2) push out, delegate responsibility for non-essential ministry, and grow in your priestly ministry to lead a parish that will begin to be transformed and will in turn transform those around it.

You need a plan for pushing out. On the following page is a basic six-month planning sheet to help you set some goals, timelines and measurements for pushing out the pastor's non-essential ministry. Complete this exercise together as a leadership team.

Push Out Plan

6-Month Planning Guide

Goals	Action Steps	Point Person	Completion Date	Measurement

If we do nothing else in the next 6 months, we must:	The single most important thing we must do in the next month is:

Parish Leadership Structures

Okay, so now you have the beginnings of a plan to free up your pastor to begin to lead change without bringing about his untimely death. Now we need to look at the leadership structures employed in your parish. In many cases, they are not just unhelpful, but are actually preventing the strategic functioning of your team.

At the beginning of this section on Being Strategic About Being Strategic, I invited you to read pages 258 to 266 in *Divine Renovation*. It wouldn't hurt at this point to go back and reread this section. It will be worth your time!

When speaking to groups of priests on this topic, the most common questions I receive are about how a leadership team operates in relationship to a pastoral council, and how a staff team fits into all of this.

Most parishes have a pastoral council or parish council of some kind, along with some staff who may or may not function as a team, or function well as a team. I believe that it is possible to not only have these groups complement one another, but also to structure them to maximize their impact on the journey from maintenance to mission.

Pastoral council

Do you remember when parish councils were cool and everyone wanted to be on them?

Well, I don't. I think this was the case for a few years in the 1970s, but not in my tenure as a priest. Some parish council meetings I have been at have been among the most boring and irrelevant meetings I have ever attended.

The source of this problem is that pastors rarely have the right model of pastoral council for the scope of the task ahead of them. Often we are not even aware of the model out of which we are working.

Take a look at the table below and identify the model you have been working out of.

Models of Parish/Pastoral Council

Composition	Focus	Driving Question
Doers	Tasks	What must be done?
Managers	Organizing	Who will do it?
Reporters	Supervision	How is it going?
Representatives	Themselves	What about us?
Passionate dreamers and planners	Strategic/big picture pastoral issues	Where are we going and how will we get there?

Questions for discussion

1) Which model, or combination of models, have you been working out of?

2) Considering the points made by Dr. Timothy Keller in his article outlined in *Divine Renovation*, what model of pastoral council do you need to move towards?

I'm sure you already know the answer to the last question. Any parish that wishes to move from maintenance to mission has to grapple with the question of where you are going and how you will get there. You need a group of people who will grapple with the big-picture pastoral issues and form a broad strategy.

In addition, every parish needs people who will carry out tasks, and people who will organize and supervise, but this should not be the focus of a parish council unless the parish is very, very small.

Every parish has self-focused (and often self-appointed) representatives, but no parish needs them. This group tends to be divisive and cares only about protecting their own turf. A parish council with this composition will never go anywhere. It will be based on suspicion and distrust, driven by self-interest.

I believe that any church with a weekend attendance of greater than 400 people needs to form a pastoral council that will focus exclusively on the question of where you are going and how you will get there.

Their goal is to articulate the parish vision and purpose and develop a broad strategy.

@SaintBP

When I became pastor at Saint Benedict Parish, the parish council was understandably composed of "reporters" (they had, after all, just completed the gargantuan task of building a brand new church building). Within a year, I led a change towards forming a pastoral council. After another year, we began work to create our parish vision and purpose statement.

For the last three years, our pastoral council has been working exclusively on five-year plans. Its focus is developing broad strategy. Lower-level strategy is formed by the leadership team and parish staff.

Our pastoral council meets once every two or three months for a full morning and is mostly composed of big-picture strategic types who have totally bought into the vision. Our leadership team members are part of the pastoral council. Our meetings are fun and energizing. We take some time to review how we are doing with the implementation of the current plan, and spend the rest of the time planning for the future.

Leadership team meetings

Any parish seeking to move from maintenance to mission will have to have a weekly leadership team meeting that focuses on tactical issues. This will be necessary because moving in this direction means you will be doing many things differently: you will be innovating, taking risks, making mistakes, evaluating and adjusting. You will no longer be in the safety of maintaining the status quo.

Your leadership team will be following the broad strategy set out by the pastoral council, which they should also be part of. The key decisions that need to be made each week are the primary focus of the leadership team.

Occasionally, an item will arise that clearly needs a deeper conversation. The conversation moves from *How should we do this?* to *Why are we doing this, anyway?* When a team moves from "how?" to "why?", the team has moved away from tactics and towards strategy. That conversation needs to take place at another time, with more than the leadership team present.

I highly recommend the book *Death by Meeting* by Patrick Lencioni. It has been a huge help to us at Saint Benedict Parish and will help your teams to have more dynamic, relevant and efficient meetings.

Is this doubling up of meetings really necessary?

Yes. If you only had a pastoral council, the team would be too large to function properly and you would have to meet every single week. This would be a huge waste of time and energy.

Why not do away with a pastoral council and just have a leadership team? While that may work in a business environment, in a parish, many parishioners would view with suspicion the sudden narrowing of influence to four or five key people (probably mostly staff), and this could cause unnecessary division. It is also my experience that it is easy for a leadership team to be so focused on the issues in front of them that they can lose touch with the parishioners "out there." Checking in with a larger group once in a while can provide a necessary corrective.

@SaintBP

Our weekly leadership team meeting is usually at least three hours long. It is the most exciting and challenging meeting of the week. After a prayer we fire up on a whiteboard topics about which a decision needs to be made. We begin by reviewing follow-up items from the previous week, then we have a brief report from each of the four staff teams on any issues that we need to know about. The rest of the meeting is spent working through the issues on the whiteboard and pushing into them until a decision has been made.

As a pastor, the things that I put up on the whiteboard involve issues that I am unclear about what to do. The discussion can be very animated. Members write all over the whiteboards in the room and we often strongly disagree. We have a nerf gun that is often employed several times each meeting.

It is important to remember that the goal of the discussion is not to reach consensus but to provide the opportunity for everyone to speak honestly and be heard. If there is no agreement, it is still my responsibility as pastor to make a decision. It is crucial that everyone does contribute and, if it is obvious, that even one member does not agree, that person is obliged to speak and not remain silent. Once a decision is made about a course of action, a point person is named and put on the accountability list for the next week.

After working out of this model for several years now, I can honestly say that "we" are making better decisions than "I" ever did. No issue is off the table. There is no decision that I have to struggle with by myself. What a relief.

Leadership is essential to the role of a priest or bishop; our Church has been dogmatically defined as hierarchical (led by priests), but if we could change the way that leadership takes place, I believe that we would be a much healthier Church. I believe that leading out of a real leadership team would be of huge significance for bishops as well.

Staff meetings

How you do staff meetings at your parish will depend entirely on the size of your staff. There is no one recipe.

If you are in a very small parish with one or two staff, your leadership team will be your staff meeting.

When you have a larger staff team, they will be distinct from your leadership team and should also meet every week.

A staff of more than 10 people will have to break up into different groups to be efficient.

@SaintBP

When I first arrived at Saint Benedict Parish, there was no weekly staff meeting. The previous pastor met with a few members of the staff every two weeks. In addition to me, we had three full-time staff, a half-time finance manager, two unpaid elderly deacons (one of whom would show up occasionally), a quarter-time music director and an elderly priest who helped out a few hours a week.

When we started to have weekly staff meetings, there were usually six of us in the meeting. After three years, there were 12 of us. At this point, we started having problems. There was not enough time to go deep enough in some areas for the meeting to be useful, and even the depth we did go to took too much time. In addition, we moved seamlessly in and out of tactics, strategy and vision.

By the time our staffing contingent was at 14, we split into staff teams. Currently, we have 22 staff, 17 of whom are paid, totalling the equivalent of 16 full-time positions and 13 full-time paid positions.

We have four staff teams: Pastoral Staff Team (7), Ops. Team (4), Clergy (5) and Communications (3). Each team meets once a week. Once a month, instead of team meetings, we have an all-staff meeting that is completely focused on vision and team building. A few staff are quarter-time positions; they do not attend meetings.

Our communications director visits each team meeting for half an hour each week, to share and gather crucial items for communication. The heads of each team and the associate pastor form the Senior Leadership Team (SLT).

The diagram below shows how the different leadership groups within Saint Benedict Parish work. It may be helpful for you to remember that we are a church with a Sunday attendance of about 1,500 to 1,800 each weekend.

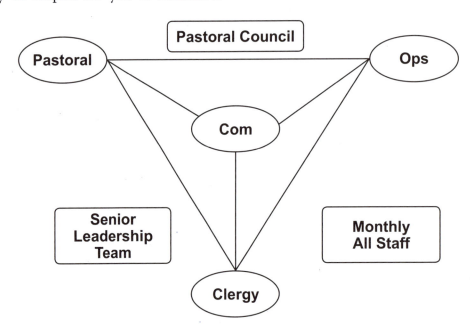

Take some time to complete the two exercise sheets on this page and the next one. Sketch out a leadership structure that would work best in your current situation so you can begin to function strategically. Next, make a plan for how you can get there over the next six months or less.

Parish Leadership Structure

Take some time below to sketch a desired structure of the leadership teams of your parish. Think outside the box.

6-Month Planning Guide

Leadership Structure

Goals	Action Steps	Point Person	Completion Date	Measurement

If we do nothing else in the next 6 months, we must:	The single most important thing we must do in the next month is:

The End and the Beginning: Vision and Assessment

Now that you are equipped to begin the journey from maintenance to mission, you no longer need to move sequentially through the chapters of this guidebook. Creating a vision and purpose statement, doing a parish assessment and creating a strategic plan take time. This is a task for your pastoral council, and it may take you more than a year to complete what is in the remainder of the next two chapters. Don't be discouraged.

I recommend that, as you move through the contents of these two chapters, you also begin to dig into Chapter 6, The Weekend, with your leadership team. That will give you a lot to chew on. If you chew quickly, and are up for it, keep on going to Chapter 5 and beyond. Once again, this chapter is for your pastoral council to work on; the remainder of the book is for your leadership team. Remember, this is not a sprint but a marathon. Don't overtax your leadership team, because they should be a key part of your pastoral council. Oh yes, you have the regular demands of parish ministry as well!

Now you are in a place to finally tackle the situation at hand. Remember the shopping mall analogy? Remember the shoes?

Let's begin by identifying your destination. This is the parish vision. As a leadership team, you have gathered around your pastor and share a common vision that is very much influenced by your pastor.

Back in Chapter 1, I asked your pastor to write down his dream for the parish in 10 years. That was a start. It was his vision and, to some degree, it is a shared and common vision. Now you must articulate it in a formal vision statement. This vision statement should be no more than a three-sentence description of the desired future of your parish.

Your diocesan bishop may or may not have articulated a vision for your diocese. Obviously, your parish vision statement must be in line with the vision of your bishop. Use your bishop's vision for the entire diocese as a guide for your discussion as well.

Here are a few suggested steps:

1) Create an initial draft version at your leadership team meeting.
2) Bring this draft to the pastoral council meeting, kick it around and make the necessary adjustments.
3) Pastoral council should facilitate meetings with ministry leaders, share the second draft with them, invite feedback and make the necessary minor adjustments.

@SaintBP

Our current Vision Statement is as follows:

Saint Benedict parish is a healthy and growing faith community that brings people to Christ, forms disciples, and sends them out to transform the world. Our members commit to worship, to grow, to serve, to connect and to give.

When I compare this to what I wrote down for my own vision of the parish, it is obviously much shorter, more succinct, but describes the same future that produced passion in me.

Parish Vision Statement
First Draft

Take some time to work out with your leadership team the first draft of a parish vision statement. Write it down below. Remember: this is a statement of what you hope and dream to be, not a description of who you are now or simply what you do or value.

Parish Vision Statement
Second Draft

After receiving feedback from the pastoral council members, write below the newest draft of your vision statement that was agreed upon at your meeting.

Parish Vision Statement
Final Version

After receiving feedback from the parish ministry leaders, write your final vision statement below.

@SaintBP

Our current Purpose Statement is as follows:

"To form disciples who joyfully live out the mission of Jesus Christ."

This is the main thing that needs to be the main thing. If we stick to this purpose, we will achieve our vision. This simple purpose statement is our compass. It brings clarity in the midst of confusion and reminds us what we ultimately must be about.

(Please note that the wording differs slightly from what is in *Divine Renovation*. That was an error on my part.)

Work with your leadership team to form a draft parish purpose statement. Keep your statement to one sentence. Go ahead, give it a try:

Work out the final version with your pastoral council. Don't skip this. It needs to come from the top.

4 The End and the Beginning: Vision and Assessment

Parish Purpose Statement
Final Version

After receiving feedback from the members of your pastoral council, write your final purpose statement below.

Communicating vision

In my somewhat limited experience of working within the Church and with pastors who have strong vision, the crucial task of communicating vision is often skipped over – with disastrous consequences.

No matter how much a vision may burn in the heart of a leader, how well he communicates it to the parish leadership, how succinctly it is written down, and how infectious he is, if the vision is not embraced by a significant portion of the parishioners, let alone heard, attempting to move the parish towards it will cause the parish to break in two.

As mentioned in *Divine Renovation*, there are no shortcuts when it comes to communicating vision: it takes time and intentionality. Vision must be communicated continuously, not simply as information, but in a way that moves hearts to desire that preferred future and be willing to make the changes necessary. Remember that vision leaks.

Take some time now as a leadership team and create a plan for the next six months for how you will communicate vision to the following people:

1) Your bishop
2) The pastoral council
3) The parish staff
4) The finance committee
5) Your ministry leaders
6) The parishioners at large

Read about communicating vision throughout your parish on pages 253–258.

Communicating Vision

Goals	Action Steps	Point Person	Completion Date	Measurement
Your Bishop				
Pastoral Council				
Parish Staff				
Finance Committee				
Ministry Leaders				
Parishioners				

If we do nothing else in the next 6 months, we must:	The single most important thing we must do in the next month is:

The most powerful tool you have in your toolbox for communicating vision is the weekend homily. That is the only time you have most of your parishioners together. Preaching about the mission of the Church and the future of your parish in a way that all your parishioners can hear and understand is essential.

This does present difficulties for some parishes that have so many Masses scheduled that it is impossible for the pastor to preach at all the Masses on any given weekend. This is truly problematic, as only the pastor can preach visioning homilies. Communicating vision is the task of the leader; it cannot be delegated to someone else.

I must be honest and say that over the last number of years, I have travelled extensively, speaking to priests in many different countries. The vast majority of priests who have a Mass schedule that makes it impossible for them to preach at every Mass have a Mass schedule that is obsolete. It remains in place out of fear of angry parishioners. Many are celebrating more than twice the number of Masses they need to be celebrating.

Let me ask you a question. Are you happy with where things are currently going in your parish? I presume, since you have made it to this point in the guidebook, that you believe there should be a slight adjustment of the course you are on. No matter how clear and compelling your vision, if you cannot speak to your whole parish, there will eventually be a big problem. If you can speak to your whole parish by changing a Mass time (or two), you will have a relatively small problem. If you can do neither, then you and your team will have to think creatively about how you do communicate at every Mass – using video, if necessary.

Do we have to use the homily for this? Yes, absolutely. No attempt to lead your church in a new direction will work unless you use the Sunday homily.

A "visioning homily" is preached at least once every three weeks at Saint Benedict Parish. This is a homily that attempts, in some way, to address the question of why are we here, where are we going and why we do the things we do, or are trying to do things we are trying to do.

As the pastor, if you find yourself in the unenviable position of desiring to lead change but have not yet been able to bi-locate in order to speak to all your parishioners on any given weekend, you and your leadership team need to seriously examine and access your Mass schedule. Use the table on the next page to obtain the information you need.

Mass Time	Seating Capacity	Average Attendance	Percentage Full

Church growth experts tell us that psychologically, a church is experienced to be full when it is at 80% capacity.

Keeping the figure of 80% in mind, do the math below and determine how many weekend Masses would make you "full."

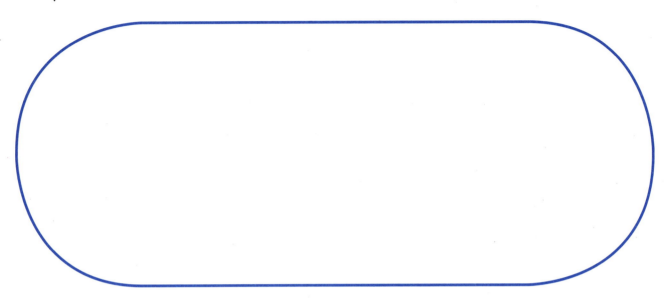

Discussion:

1) If anything was possible, what weekend schedule would allow your pastor to preach at all Masses?

2) How many Masses do you really need? (Keep in mind that you will want room for growth eventually, but your primary goal at this point is to enable the pastor to speak to all your parishioners on one weekend.)

3) What Mass schedule will best allow you to achieve these goals?

Take some time on the next page to make a plan about how you will communicate about this change and carry it out. The fact that the pastor desires to speak to all the parishioners will itself be a compelling reason for many parishioners. Not all, mind you, but many.

Mass Schedule

6-Month Planning Guide

Goals	Action Steps	Point Person	Completion Date	Measurement

If we do nothing else in the next 6 months, we must:	The single most important thing we must do in the next month is:

Go to divinerenovation.net. Under Media, go to Exploring themes and watch the second video, entitled "Leadership and Vision." Begin at the 7:30 mark.

Congratulations!

Now, here's some bad news. Fasten your seatbelt. As soon as you even hint that you are about to touch the most underattended Mass, there will be pushback. If you make any changes around Mass times, you will receive complaints. Some people will even leave the parish.

Here's the point.

If you implement this guidebook, people are going to leave your parish. Do you know why? Because although parishioners want change, they don't want to change.

Nothing unmasks the unhealthy spiritual consumerism that grips our Church like the McDonaldsization of our Mass schedules. Go ahead: touch them and see what happens.

Here's the question for you and your leadership team.

What will you do when the complaints begin to come in? Will you allow those who make the most noise to bring this first stage of change to a grinding halt? Sadly, many kind-hearted, well-meaning pastors do.

Why don't you agree right now as a team to stick together through this one. You know that changing nothing is not an option, so what's the worst that could happen? Okay, realistically, what's the worst that could happen? Go ahead – write it down.

What's the Worst that Can Happen?

You might as well be prepared to help each other through the storm. Be prepared to endure it and hold each other to what was decided.

Sign below and pledge to weather the storm:

The truth is that any change will make people upset. If you undertake this journey, you will lose parishioners. This is the test case for what lies ahead. Can you do it?

You may remember that at the beginning of this book, I mentioned how after five years we had returned to the same number of parishioners we had at the beginning of my tenure as pastor. After five years, over 50% of our current parishioners had not been part of the original three parishes that came together.

How can this be? What happened to them? We are talking about at least 800 people. Well, they left. Some moved away to other parts of the city or country. We have about 60 funerals a year and at least half were churchgoers (that certainly adds up), but the rest left because, in some way, they chose to no longer belong because of the changes that were made. I am not willing to judge whether they were justified in doing so. They made their own decision and God bless them. Most left quietly, but many made a lot of noise.

As I said at the beginning, it has all been worth it. Our attendance is back up, we have 40% involvement in discipleship, and our liturgies are much more dynamic. Our collection has doubled, hundreds of lives have been changed, our pews are full of people who have had conversions, and ministry is flourishing, with more than half our adults in some form of ministry.

It is worth the pain.

I am often asked, "How did you deal with the negativity and pushback?" The honest answer is, not very well – at least, at first.

In the first year I read every complaint, anonymous and otherwise. If I received angry phone messages, I played them over and over again. I engaged with angry emails, even those from newly created anonymous accounts. I agonized, shed a few tears, and got angry and frustrated.

As time went on, though, I became more discerning about how to engage negative feedback with the help of those around me.

Read about dealing with negativity and pushback in the section entitled "Having a Thick Skin" on pages 279–281.

Below, I offer a few questions for discerning pushback.

1) Is it anonymous?

When I finally smartened up and stopped reading anonymous communications, I told parishioners that I simply would not read such things. My secretary opens any letter that is without a return address. If it is anonymous, she does not even tell me it came in. I don't need to know. To be honest, they still bother me enough to ruin a part of my day or distract me as I'm heading to an important meeting.

2) Is the person on board with the vision?

Okay, so it's not anonymous. I will read it, but how much weight should I give it? This next question is simple. Is this person rowing for the same shore that we are? If the answer is no, I do not engage with the ideas presented (it's not worth the energy). I thank the person for their feedback (at least they put their name on it) and wish them well. The fundamental direction of our parish is not up for grabs. If the answer is yes, however, I proceed to the next question.

3) Has the person bought in?

So it's not anonymous and the person desires to go in the same direction. The next question is to determine if this person is just all words. How do you determine this? Easy. Are they involved in discipleship? Do they serve in ministry? What about their financial giving? In my experience, the people who make the most noise about withdrawing their financial support are the ones who give the least. Check it and see. If the person has not bought in, once again thank him or her for the feedback, give it some consideration, but don't worry about it too much. If the person has bought in, this feedback needs some serious consideration. If it is simply a tactical issue, an adjustment could then be made according to the feedback.

4) Is it theologically based?

This next question is key as you grapple with feedback. A person may have feedback that is simply procedural. This certainly deserves attention and response. However, listen for a theological reason. If the person has a point and it is rooted theologically, this will be something you need to bring to your leadership team. Another possibility is that the issue is simply a matter of personal preference. If so, I would not expend too much energy on it.

5) Can I build the parish around this person?

Sometimes even good people who are on board make good solid points, but in the end, after discussion and consideration, you must stay the course. In times like this, it is possible to lose such a key parishioner (people leave parishes for a whole range of reasons, and are more likely to do so in larger parishes). This question seems rather mercenary, but it is necessary to ask. Is this person contagious? Is it worth it to make a compromise or adjustment, that you may not feel is necessary, in order to keep this person on board? Can you risk losing this person?

@SaintBP

We often face this question when amazing parishioners come to us with great ideas. So often, great ideas are a menace to the best ideas. You simply cannot run after every great idea in a parish, especially if you are being intentional and focused. Saying no to such parishioners is a risk, but one that needs to be carefully assessed.

Perhaps the flowchart on the next page will help you discern how to respond to pushback.

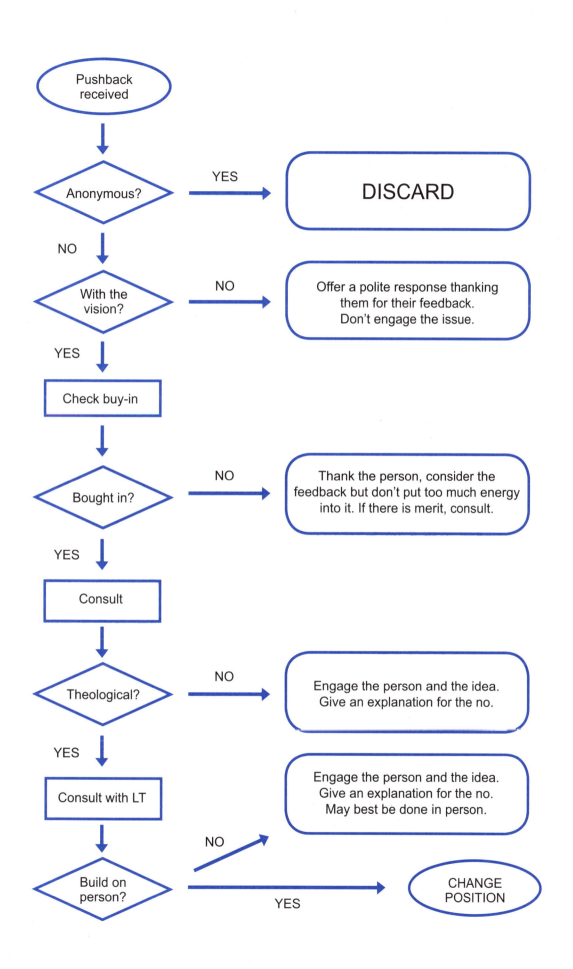

@SaintBP

"Haters Gonna Hate," October 14, 2015 – by Fr. Simon Lobo, C.C.

Chances are that if you are out front, leading with innovation, sooner or later you will get arrows in your back (or your butt... or both). As priests, we know this to be true. I am sure that all of us have an arsenal of complaint stories. One of the most "impressive" critiques that I received years ago was from someone who did not appreciate that my preaching was so joyful. They went to the trouble of creating an anonymous email account (something like *fromafriend@hotmail.com*) to share their concerns with me. They even sent me video clips of an adversarial Catholic media personality enthusiastically describing all of the ways that I had been deviating from orthodox Catholicism (I had to pull out the dictionary a few times to comprehend some of the more remarkable vocabulary words). I can laugh about it now, but at the time it really bothered me.

This past weekend, after preaching about Jesus' response to the man to "Go, sell what you have, and give to the poor" (Mk 10:17-30), I was accosted by a relatively polite, but firm, lady who had a "theological disagreement" with me. As she saw it, Jesus was in no way suggesting that we need to be financially generous. Instead, he was merely asking us to give a little of our time. Furthermore, she told me that she knew a lot of very nice rich people. Ultimately, I think she was just annoyed that I had the audacity to talk about money at church (no doubt spoiling her Canadian Thanksgiving weekend). I cannot say that I enjoy that kind of contrary energy coming at me, and often, after the fact, I think of better ways I could have responded. Nevertheless, as I reflected on the encounter, I laughed to myself when I realized that only one person complained (as it turns out, she was a visitor). Kudos to FJM and the team for creating a culture at SBP whereby money is a part of normal discourse.

Keenly aware that criticism is something that I find difficult to deal with – which can easily deflate me – I brought it up in one of my first 1-on-1 meetings with FJM. I asked, "How do you deal with criticism?" His response: "Not very well." That being said, he has improved considerably in this area from when he was first ordained. He has developed a kind of flow chart to filter through the plethora of complaints. Firstly, if the administrative assistant receives an anonymous letter, she shreds it without even telling FJM that it came in. The next filtering criteria have to do with the vision and the big picture strategy. If a person is quick to criticize but is not united with the parish vision and has made little effort to participate in the overall parish strategy, then a polite "Thank you" is in order, but the comments are not given much credence. Patrick Lencioni differentiates between the "strategic" and the "tactical" (the latter dealing more with the day-to-day decisions and issues). If a parishioner is on board with the vision, involved in the strategy, and has some suggestions to offer (perhaps with regards to

a particular tactical approach), that person deserves FJM's attention. He might sit down with them to hear them out. They might even offer ideas that are very legitimate and worthy of consideration and implementation.

What do I want you to know?

If we really hope to bring our parishes and ministries to a place where they are having a powerful impact on the people within and the people on the outside, we can expect to receive pushback. Newton's *Law of Inertia* comes into play: objects at rest like to stay at rest. The same can be said of dormant Catholics.

What do I want you to do?

Brace yourself for the inevitable negativity. Speak with your staff or volunteers, who are on the front lines, to develop a basic approach for dealing with complaints. In order to properly discern if a person's criticism is worth your time, it is crucial to clarify the vision. I would hope that every Catholic parish or ministry sees themselves as a place where missionary disciples are in abundance. If a critic is fully in line with this vision (and a respective strategy to bring this about), then be open to receiving his or her insights with humility.

Back to the shopping mall

So, now everyone knows that you want to buy new shoes and they know where the shoe store is. A few people didn't want new shoes and they are off to the food court. That's sad, but you know you really need new shoes.

Before you start putting more miles on your old shoes, you need to make a plan to be able to get there. The next step in this process is to find the YOU ARE HERE dot to determine where you are actually starting from. This is about assessment.

Let's begin with a values analysis

I make the case in *Divine Renovation* that values shape culture and that values that are actually lived and not just aspirational make that culture healthy or unhealthy. Healthy things bear fruit and grow. Unhealthy things decline and die. The problem with the lack of fruit in many of our parishes is a lack of health. The soil condition is the problem, not the tree.

 Read about the various assessment exercises you can engage in with your pastoral council on pages 267–271.

Luke 13:6-9   The Parable of the Barren Fig Tree

"A man had a fig tree planted in his vineyard; and he came looking for fruit on it and found none. So he said to the gardener, 'See here! For three years I have come looking for fruit on this fig tree, and still I find none. Cut it down! Why should it be wasting the soil?' He replied, 'Sir, let it alone for one more year, until I dig around it and put manure on it. If it bears fruit next year, well and good; but if not, you can cut it down.'"

A values analysis is about a brutally honest assessment of the soil condition of your parish. You will look at behaviours, for what we do reflects what we truly value. This analysis has two parts:

1) A brutally honest admission of what your current real values are.
2) An evaluation of where you are in relation to the 10 values that create health (don't be discouraged, none of us are there yet).

Are you ready?

Use the exercise on the following page with your pastoral council. You may want to invite ministry leaders and other key parishioners to provide their feedback.

A large part of the book is devoted to examining the 10 values that lead to health. You can find these in Chapter 5, "Laying the Foundation," on pages 87–195.

Go to divinerenovation.net. Under Media, go to "Exploring themes" and watch the fourth video, entitled "The Importance of Culture."

What do we truly value?

This is a tough one. Get your budget, your parish schedule and your booking list and let them tell you what you really value in your parish. Discuss and pay attention to stay away from aspirational values. They can come later. Be brutally honest about how what you do, as opposed to what you say, reveals your actual values. Write them down below.

Ten Values Analysis

The only place to start is where you are. Use the questions below, based on Chapter 5 of *Divine Renovation*, to clarify your point of departure. Once again, be honest and determine your starting point by responding to the five questions for each value, then add up your total.

3=Usually   2=Sometimes   1=Rarely   0=Never

1. Giving Priority to the Weekend

a) More time is spent by the pastor and key staff on the weekend experience than on the rest of the week.
b) The Sunday Mass is a Wow moment for parishioners.
c) Our Mass schedule gives us sufficient time to gather, celebrate the Eucharist and connect afterwards.
d) People are unconcerned about going over the sacred 1-hour mark and turning into pumpkins.
e) Our building(s) facilitate a meaningful and transformative Sunday experience.

Total: _____

2. Hospitality

a) We have a dedicated and trained hospitality team in our parish.
b) At parish social events, parishioners go out of their way to welcome people they do not know.
c) The marginalized (the poor, people with mental illness, etc.) are intentionally welcomed in our parish.
d) We have an intentional welcoming process for new parishioners in our parish.
e) It is obvious to visitors that we presume that we have non-churchgoers, non-Catholics and visitors at every weekend Mass.

Total: _____

3. Uplifting Music

a) We have an excellent level of congregational singing in our church.
b) We have a high quality of music in our Sunday liturgies.
c) We have a good mix of old and new styles of music at different Masses.
d) We are intentional about developing contemporary music.
e) The hymn of praise has a primary place in our liturgies.

Total: _____

4. Great Homilies

a) The preachers in our parish speak to the whole person: mind, heart, conscience and will.
b) Every homily clearly enunciates the Kerygma.
c) Preaching, however challenging, feels like good news.
d) Preaching in our parish is truly transformative and relevant.
e) The pastor preaches a visioning homily at least once a month at all Masses.

Total: _____

5. Meaningful Community

a) In our parish, parishioners are accountable to and for one another.
b) A majority of our parishioners regularly participate in a small or mid-size group.
c) Our parish facilitates experiences of belonging for people who neither believe nor behave as we would wish them to.
d) In our parish, people are known by name.
e) At our parish, we seek to grow a sense of belonging by measuring it.

Total: _____

6. Clear Expectations

a) Our parishioners know what is expected of them as members of our parish.
b) Our parishioners know what they can expect from our parish.
c) We have clearly defined and articulated these expectations.
d) At our parish we do a great job of holding the value of clear expectations in creative tension with the value of hospitality.
e) We have annual initiatives when these expectations are revisited and communicated at all the Masses.

Total: _____

7. Strengths-Based Ministry

a) We use our church to build up people and not people to build up our church.
b) We have a defined tool to help parishioners discover their God-given strengths and talents.
c) When matching people to ministry, we begin with the person and not with the need.
d) Key teams in our parish are composed intentionally using a strengths assessment tool of some kind.
e) Serving in and through our parish is always life-giving and energizing.

Total: _____

8. Formation of Small Communities

a) Our parish is a community of communities where people are known, loved and cared for.
b) We have a defined system of small and/or mid-sized groups in our parish, and belonging to them is considered a normal part of being a parishioner.
c) After evangelization, getting people into small and/or mid-sized groups is our top pastoral priority.
d) The ministries and groups in our parish do not depend on the direct oversight of the pastor.
e) Caring for one another spiritually is the responsibility of all, and not just of the pastor.

Total: _____

9. Experience of the Holy Spirit

a) The majority of our parishioners can testify to a powerful experience of the Holy Spirit.
b) In our parish liturgies and gatherings, we always explicitly invoke the Holy Spirit in prayer and in song.
c) We have a working model so that parishioners can be prayed over to have an experience of being filled with the Holy Spirit.
d) In our parish we discern but also welcome various manifestations and gifts of the Holy Spirit.
e) In our staff meetings and pastoral council meetings we invoke and wait upon the Holy Spirit.

Total: _____

10. An Invitational Church

a) In our parish, parishioners are comfortable inviting family, friends and neighbours to church events.
b) A culture of invitation is supported by regular teaching and preaching by the pastor.
c) Parishioners are confident that the experience of the weekend will be relevant and uplifting for their unchurched friends and family members.
d) Outside of the weekend Masses, we have events in our parish that are intentionally designed to host the unchurched.
e) We celebrate wins through stories of both invitations made and invitations responded to.

Total: _____

Ten Values Assessment Scoring

Total up your average score for each value and rank them, giving a 1 to your highest score.

Value	Average Total Score	Rank
Priority to the weekend		
Hospitality		
Uplifting music		
Great homilies		
Meaningful community		
Clear expectations		
Strengths-based ministry		
Formation of small communities		
Experience of the Holy Spirit		
An invitational Church		

4 The End and the Beginning: Vision and Assessment

I know that that was a heavy one to lay on you. Cheer up! No parish that I know of has a perfect score on all of these.

If truth be told, the sad reality is that too many churches would score a 5 or less in every single category. Be encouraged if you are scoring between a 5 and a 10, and give thanks to God for the areas where you are between a 10 and a 15.

Take some time to discuss this exercise with your leadership team.

Questions for discussion

1) How do you feel about the exercise you have just undertaken?

2) Were you surprised by what you learned? How?

3) Were there major differences of opinion about your assessment of any of the ten values?

4) Where are you strongest?

5) Where are you weakest?

Okay, the first thing is not to be discouraged. Honest self-assessment is the best place from which to begin. Evaluating the health of our parish by comparing ourselves to neighbouring churches is not very helpful. The good news is that perhaps you now can see a little more clearly.

Don't be overwhelmed. As someone once said, the best way to eat an elephant is one bite at a time. By working hard and being intentional, you will begin to see some change within months. You will see substantial change in three years and be well on the way to becoming a missionary parish.

Now you need to make a plan based on this data.

The first four of these values are rooted in the weekend experience. Chances are that you have already put a plan in place to tackle these, as your leadership team has already started working on Chapter 4. If you have not yet begun to focus on the weekend experience, then this is your top priority.

Outside of the values related to the weekend experience, pick one other area for your leadership team to work on in the coming six months. You can chip away at that one value while you continue to do the work in the pages ahead on a full five-year plan.

You may wish to begin with the value that is your weakest, or you may begin with the one that is the most strategic at this point in your journey.

Use the six-month planning sheet on the following page.

Remember, as you set goals and objectives, don't just plan to execute but also to communicate the "why?"

6-Month Planning Guide

Value:_____

Goals	Action Steps	Point Person	Completion Date	Measurement

If we do nothing else in the next 6 months, we must:

The single most important thing we must do in the next month is:

The ME25 evaluation

Another option your parish may wish to engage in is Gallup's ME25 evaluation. We have been using this tool for six years at Saint Benedict Parish and find it very useful.

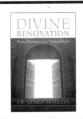
Read about Gallup philosophy, engagement and the ME25 survey in parishes on pages 149–153.

I highly recommend that parishes seriously consider this tool. It is like getting your blood work done when you go to the doctor. Besides getting measurements in the three categories of engaged, unengaged and actively disengaged parishioners, leadership teams will receive a plethora of data that is research based and highly useful for pastoral planning.

Parishes will receive a complete breakdown of the 25 questions, along with a comparison to all Catholic churches in the database and to all churches together. The survey provides a great deal of demographic information that, over time, allows you to see how your membership is changing. The test results also come with various options for coaching and help with analyzing, interpreting and applying the results.

The most important benefit of this survey is the repeated use of this metric over the years. As you continue to track your vitals, you measure your growth in health while you implement your strategy.

There is a cost involved in this, but I believe that it is money well spent. If the structural integrity of the church building was in question, I doubt that any parish would hesitate to pay to have regular assessments done on the building.

To find out more about the ME25 survey, or to arrange a survey for your parish, go to gallup.com: choose Online Products and then Faith Member Engagement.

ME25 Survey Results

Use the space below to record your results over the next number of years that you choose to use this tool. Record the date when the survey was administered, your basic scores, and finally, your ratio of engaged to actively disengaged. Remember, the soil becomes healthy at 4:1.

DATE	% ENGAGED	% UNENGAGED	% ACTIVELY DISENGAGED	HEALTH RATIO

The End and the Beginning: Vision and Assessment

The Plan:
You Need a Vision *and* a Plan

In the previous chapter, you created a common vision statement, established a clear purpose and identified your starting point by checking the vital signs of life in your parish. In this chapter we will finally build a plan with your pastoral council. We will begin with an exercise that will form the foundation of your five-year strategic plan.

Read about the Five Systems Analysis on pages 269–271.

I know that you have already peeked ahead at the rest of this chapter and may have thought some unkind thoughts about me. First, what lies ahead is much easier than it may look at first glance. Second, it's going to take you most of the next year to complete this exercise, so don't be overwhelmed. Third, you are not doing this alone. You will be working with your pastoral council, which by this time is full of competent strategic, big-picture people who absolutely love doing this kind of thing.

Before you proceed, it is vital that the members of your pastoral council have a common understanding of each system. Never presume that, just because you use the same word, you are working out of a common understanding.

Take some time on the next page to create a one- or two-sentence definition of each system. I encourage you to reflect closely the core meanings found in *Divine Renovation*, but use your own words. Although every system is interconnected and interdependent, be clear in your definitions so that each system is distinct from the other.

Five Systems Definitions

WORSHIP	
EVANGELIZATION	
DISCIPLESHIP	
FELLOWSHIP/ COMMUNITY	
MINISTRY	

Mini-visions

This is not about hallucinations, but about specific short-term visions. What do I mean? Well, vision is where you are going – a picture of the future that makes you passionate.

Stop and write down today's date:

_____

Write down the date five years from now:

_____

How old will you be? How old will your children be? How will your favourite baseball team be doing (or hockey team, if you live in Canada)?

Now think about the experience of worship in your parish five years from now. What would it have to look like to make you incredibly excited?

What about evangelization? What about discipleship and community? What is happening in the world of ministry in five years that makes you incredibly excited?

Is this just a repetition of what we did in the last chapter when we formed the parish vision statement? No, it's not. That big vision, if it was suitably big, may be a future that you never reach, even though you continue to move towards it year after year. Your mini-visions are more realistic, kind of…

Okay, start describing them on the following pages.

5 The Plan: You Need a Vision *and* a Plan

Five-Year Vision for Worship

Five years from now the experience of worship at your parish makes you incredibly excited. What is happening? What does it look like? Remember, you are describing the entire weekend experience and not just the liturgy itself.

Five-Year Vision for Evangelization

Five years from now your parish has begun to mobilize, and churchgoers and non-churchgoers are encountering Jesus and making decisions to follow him as his disciples. What does it all look like? Describe it below.

Five-Year Vision for Discipleship

Five years from now your parish is doing a great job of helping those who have been renewed in faith to grow and mature as disciples. What does it look like? Describe it below.

Five-Year Vision for Community

Five years from now your parish has taken great strides to be a place where people are welcomed, known, loved and supported in their Christian faith. What does this look like? Be specific. Write it down.

Five-Year Vision for Ministry

Five years from now your parish is known to be a place where ministry is flourishing – within the walls of your church and out in the community. Describe what is happening. Write it down.

SWOT analysis

So now you have agreed upon definitions and an exciting description of what your parish will look like in five years. This is awesome! Are you excited? I hope you are.

Do you know what? What you have written is doable. Others have done it, and so can you. The same Holy Spirit who has brought renewed life to so many other churches also wants to bring life to your church. Let's keep going.

The next step is to conduct a SWOT analysis of each of the five systems to explore your strengths, weaknesses, opportunities and threats. You may want to break your team into smaller groups if this is beneficial. The goal is to get as much input as possible in the most efficient manner.

SWOT exercise sheets are provided on the following pages. Use them to get the ideas down on paper. Later you will have a chance to eliminate redundancies, summarize and clarify. For now, this is an organized brainstorming session.

We are going to use this information to help you assemble the elements of a five-year strategic plan, and then give you the tools you need to build that plan. Don't be overwhelmed by what lies ahead. All of this takes time.

Worship SWOT Analysis

What are your current strengths, weaknesses, opportunities and threats in the area of worship in your parish as defined by your team?

Strengths | **Weaknesses**

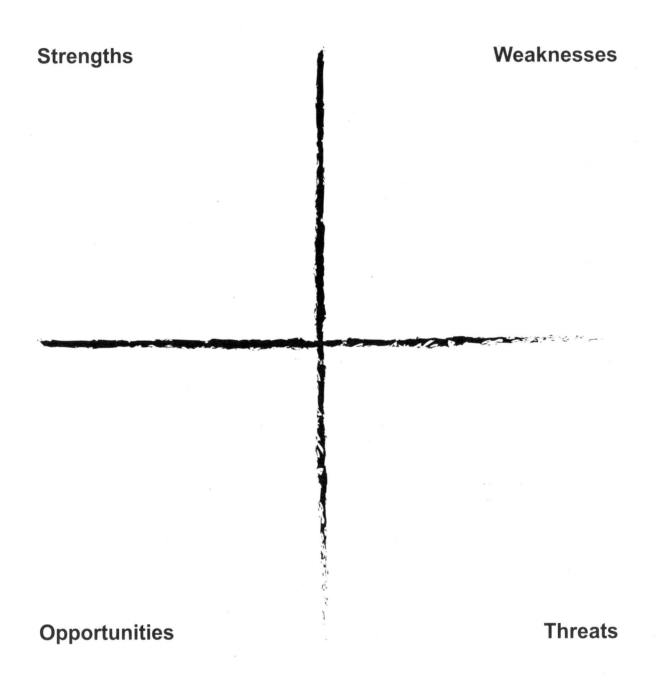

Opportunities | **Threats**

Evangelization SWOT Analysis

What are your current strengths, weaknesses, opportunities and threats in the area of evangelization in your parish as defined by your team?

Strengths | **Weaknesses**

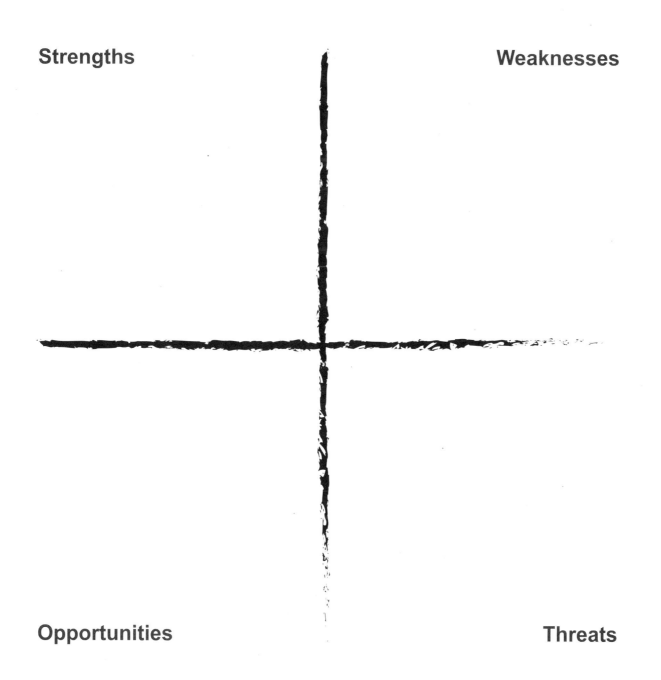

Opportunities | **Threats**

Discipleship SWOT Analysis

What are your current strengths, weaknesses, opportunities and threats in the area of discipleship in your parish as defined by your team?

Strengths	**Weaknesses**
Opportunities	**Threats**

Fellowship SWOT Analysis

What are your current strengths, weaknesses, opportunities and threats in the area of fellowship in your parish as defined by your team?

Strengths **Weaknesses**

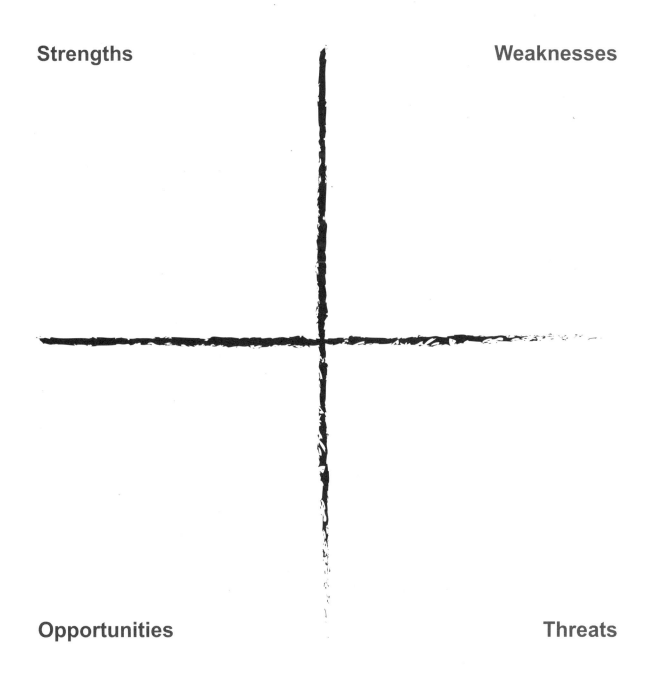

Opportunities **Threats**

Ministry SWOT Analysis

What are your current strengths, weaknesses, opportunities and threats in the area of ministry in your parish as defined by your team?

Strengths | **Weaknesses**

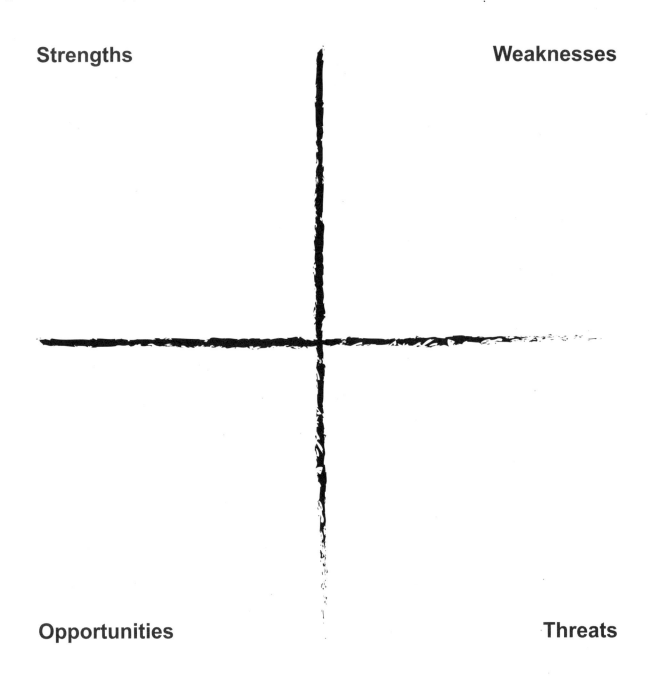

Opportunities | **Threats**

Clarification and reflection

Congratulations on the brainstorming session! I hope you had a lot of fun and lots of laughs.

In the pages ahead, you are going to have the opportunity to summarize the analysis of each system. Eliminate duplications and group closely related elements.

After you bring order to your work, you will find a set of questions on each of the five systems. Take your time with these and be sure to write your answers in the space provided.

Worship SWOT Summary

Summarize your analysis of the present state of worship in your parish.

Strengths

Weaknesses

Opportunities

Threats

Questions for discussion on the state of worship in your parish

1) What strength do you have in this area that you could easily build on?

2) Among the weaknesses you listed, what would be the easiest one to fix?

3) What is your greatest weakness?

4) What is your greatest opportunity? What one thing has the greatest potential for the least amount of time and resources?

5) What is your most immediate threat (short-term)?

6) What is your greatest threat (the one that could cause the greatest harm)?

Evangelization SWOT Summary

Summarize your analysis of the present state of evangelization in your parish.

Strengths

Weaknesses

Opportunities

Threats

Questions for discussion on the state of evangelization in your parish

1) What strength do you have in this area that you could easily build on?

2) Among the weaknesses you listed, what would be the easiest one to fix?

3) What is your greatest weakness?

4) What is your greatest opportunity? What one thing has the greatest potential for the least amount of time and resources?

5) What is your most immediate threat (short-term)?

6) What is your greatest threat (the one that could cause the greatest harm)?

Discipleship SWOT Summary

Summarize your analysis of the present state of discipleship in your parish.

Strengths

Weaknesses

Opportunities

Threats

Questions for discussion on the state of discipleship in your parish

1) What strength do you have in this area that you could easily build on?

2) Among the weaknesses you listed, what would be the easiest one to fix?

3) What is your greatest weakness?

4) What is your greatest opportunity? What one thing has the greatest potential for the least amount of time and resources?

5) What is your most immediate threat (short-term)?

6) What is your greatest threat (the one that could cause the greatest harm)?

Community SWOT Summary

Summarize your analysis of the present state of community in your parish.

Strengths

Weaknesses

Opportunities

Threats

Questions for discussion on the state of community in your parish

1) What strength do you have in this area that you could easily build on?

2) Among the weaknesses you listed, what would be the easiest one to fix?

3) What is your greatest weakness?

4) What is your greatest opportunity? What one thing has the greatest potential for the least amount of time and resources?

5) What is your most immediate threat (short-term)?

6) What is your greatest threat (the one that could cause the greatest harm)?

Ministry SWOT Summary

Summarize your analysis of the present state of ministry in your parish.

Strengths

Weaknesses

Opportunities

Threats

Questions for discussion on the state of ministry in your parish

1) What strength do you have in this area that you could easily build on?

2) Among the weaknesses you listed, what would be the easiest one to fix?

3) What is your greatest weakness?

4) What is your greatest opportunity? What one thing has the greatest potential for the least amount of time and resources?

5) What is your most immediate threat (short-term)?

6) What is your greatest threat (the one that could cause the greatest harm)?

@SaintBP

All the exercises we have described in these pages around forming a vision and purpose statement, assessment and the five systems analysis and visioning took us about a year for our pastoral council to complete. Don't be discouraged. What you are doing will impact your parish for the next 20 years or more. Lives will be transformed and eternities will be impacted.

The Mini-plan

I know what you are thinking. Mini-plan? When are we going to get to the BIG plan?

I ask you to trust me and be patient. In the months to come, you and your team are going to build a wonderful plan. Think of the analogy of building something made of Lego. Before you can do this, you need Lego blocks.

In the exercise that follows, you are going to create 20 different blocks with which to build your plan.

No, I'm not kidding. Don't worry, it will likely take you another six months of planning before you finish your BIG five-year plan, and then you only have to tackle four things each year when you begin to implement it. You can do this!

Okay, so here's what we're going to do:

Use the planning outline on the next page to create a different mini-plan for each quadrant of the SWOT analysis. Use your mini-vision statements, your summaries and your discussion notes as points of reference.

Use these four questions to form your mini-plans:

1) The one **strength** that you can easily build on.
2) Your easiest **weakness** to fix.
3) The **opportunity** with the greatest potential that you can exploit for the least investment.
4) The greatest **threat** you should address, either short-term or long-term.

Each exercise sheet has room for three goals. You do not need to come up with three, but definitely don't create more than three. Stay focused on the *one* item you have identified as the most important. This will give you enough to work on in the coming years. Remember, you can do a lot in five years, but you can't do everything.

It may be helpful if you can break your pastoral council into five different teams and assign each team to a different system. Your call.

For now, think of each mini-plan as almost self-contained. The time frames in the small boxes at the bottom of each sheet refer to one month or six months after you begin to implement that particular plan.

Once you complete this exercise, you and your team will have the building blocks to create a mini-plan to move this system of parish life into a place of health.

6-Month Planning Guide

System: WorshipSWOT Quadrant: Strength

Goals	Action Steps	Point Person	Completion Date	Measurement

If we do nothing else in the next 6 months, we must:	The single most important thing we must do in the next month is:

6-Month Planning Guide

System: WorshipSWOT Quadrant: Weakness

Goals	Action Steps	Point Person	Completion Date	Measurement

If we do nothing else in the next 6 months, we must:	The single most important thing we must do in the next month is:

6-Month Planning Guide

System: Worship **SWOT Quadrant:** Opportunity

Goals	Action Steps	Point Person	Completion Date	Measurement

If we do nothing else in the next 6 months, we must:	The single most important thing we must do in the next month is:

6-Month Planning Guide

System: Worship **SWOT Quadrant:** Threat

Goals	Action Steps	Point Person	Completion Date	Measurement

If we do nothing else in the next 6 months, we must:	The single most important thing we must do in the next month is:

5 The Plan: You Need a Vision *and* a Plan

6-Month Planning Guide

System: Evangelization SWOT Quadrant: Strength

Goals	Action Steps	Point Person	Completion Date	Measurement

If we do nothing else in the next 6 months, we must:	The single most important thing we must do in the next month is:

6-Month Planning Guide

System: Evangelization SWOT Quadrant: Weakness

Goals	Action Steps	Point Person	Completion Date	Measurement

If we do nothing else in the next 6 months, we must:	The single most important thing we must do in the next month is:

6-Month Planning Guide

System: Evangelization   **SWOT Quadrant:** Opportunity

Goals	Action Steps	Point Person	Completion Date	Measurement

If we do nothing else in the next 6 months, we must:	The single most important thing we must do in the next month is:

6-Month Planning Guide

System: Evangelization   **SWOT Quadrant:** Threat

Goals	Action Steps	Point Person	Completion Date	Measurement

If we do nothing else in the next 6 months, we must:	The single most important thing we must do in the next month is:

6-Month Planning Guide

System: Discipleship SWOT Quadrant: Strength

Goals	Action Steps	Point Person	Completion Date	Measurement

If we do nothing else in the next 6 months, we must:	The single most important thing we must do in the next month is:

6-Month Planning Guide

System: Discipleship SWOT Quadrant: Weakness

Goals	Action Steps	Point Person	Completion Date	Measurement

If we do nothing else in the next 6 months, we must:	The single most important thing we must do in the next month is:

6-Month Planning Guide

System: Discipleship   SWOT Quadrant: Opportunity

Goals	Action Steps	Point Person	Completion Date	Measurement

If we do nothing else in the next 6 months, we must:	The single most important thing we must do in the next month is:

6-Month Planning Guide

System: Discipleship   SWOT Quadrant: Threat

Goals	Action Steps	Point Person	Completion Date	Measurement

If we do nothing else in the next 6 months, we must:	The single most important thing we must do in the next month is:

5 · The Plan: You Need a Vision *and* a Plan

6-Month Planning Guide

System: Community   SWOT Quadrant: Strength

Goals	Action Steps	Point Person	Completion Date	Measurement

If we do nothing else in the next 6 months, we must:	The single most important thing we must do in the next month is:

6-Month Planning Guide

System: Community   SWOT Quadrant: Weakness

Goals	Action Steps	Point Person	Completion Date	Measurement

If we do nothing else in the next 6 months, we must:	The single most important thing we must do in the next month is:

6-Month Planning Guide

System: <u>Community</u>   **SWOT Quadrant:** <u>Opportunity</u>

Goals	Action Steps	Point Person	Completion Date	Measurement

If we do nothing else in the next 6 months, we must:	The single most important thing we must do in the next month is:

6-Month Planning Guide

System: <u>Community</u>   **SWOT Quadrant:** <u>Threat</u>

Goals	Action Steps	Point Person	Completion Date	Measurement

If we do nothing else in the next 6 months, we must:	The single most important thing we must do in the next month is:

5 The Plan: You Need a Vision *and* a Plan

6-Month Planning Guide

System: Ministry   SWOT Quadrant: Strength

Goals	Action Steps	Point Person	Completion Date	Measurement

If we do nothing else in the next 6 months, we must:	The single most important thing we must do in the next month is:

6-Month Planning Guide

System: Ministry   SWOT Quadrant: Weakness

Goals	Action Steps	Point Person	Completion Date	Measurement

If we do nothing else in the next 6 months, we must:	The single most important thing we must do in the next month is:

6-Month Planning Guide

System: <u>Ministry</u>   **SWOT Quadrant:** <u>Opportunity</u>

Goals	Action Steps	Point Person	Completion Date	Measurement

If we do nothing else in the next 6 months, we must:	The single most important thing we must do in the next month is:

6-Month Planning Guide

System: <u>Ministry</u>   **SWOT Quadrant:** <u>Threat</u>

Goals	Action Steps	Point Person	Completion Date	Measurement

If we do nothing else in the next 6 months, we must:	The single most important thing we must do in the next month is:

5   The Plan: You Need a Vision *and* a Plan

Building a plan

Let's again think of the Lego blocks. Now you have 20 of them. It's time to assemble them.

This phase of planning will be crucial. I recommend that you take a full day with your pastoral council and begin with an extended time of prayer. This one is going to take more than just human wisdom.

The first thing you need to do is to determine the time frame for each year. In the business world, it is normal to go by the calendar year. In the ministry world, it is common to follow the academic year, from September to August.

You are going to arrange your building blocks and then fill in the table on the next page. Resist the temptation to begin implementing everything at once. This will be a rolling plan and will be cumulative.

What do I mean? Well, as you begin to implement the second round of mini-plans, you have to keep the first round moving forward.

Before you panic, remember that *implementation and execution* is not the responsibility of your pastoral council, but of your leadership team, staff and the key ministry leaders they support. Remember, pastoral council focuses on BIG-picture pastoral plan and broad strategy, and the leadership team oversees lower-end strategy and tactics. Staff and ministry leaders execute.

Below is an example of what you might prepare. It's just an example; don't overanalyze it.

2017–18	2018–19	2019–20	2020–21	2021–22
Worship Strength	Worship Weakness	Community Strength	Discipleship Opportunity	Discipleship Weakness
Evangelization Opportunity	Evangelization Threat	Evangelization Strength	Evangelization Weakness	Ministry Weakness
Community Threat	Discipleship Strength	Ministry Opportunity	Community Opportunity	Discipleship Threat
Worship Threat	Worship Opportunity	Community Weakness	Ministry Strength	Ministry Threat

Map Your Five-Year Plan

Put your 20 mini-plans into your time frame and begin to give shape to your five-year plan. Work it out as a team and put your final results on this sheet.

The problem with five-year plans is that they are *five*-year plans. You are planning to implement change, and when you change things, things change. In truth, most five-year plans are only good for about three years.

So why bother? Well, you do need a framework. Pastoral planning will always have to be updated at key points. Things may look very different three years from now. Guess what? You have three years before you have to worry about that.

Let's look more closely at what you have prepared and focus on the next three years.

Detailed three-year plan

Remember the mini-planning sheets? We are now going to collate and chart out your specific goals for each year. Imagine that you actually set three goals for each of the 20 mini-plans.

If I was working with the fake five-year plan that I mapped out on page 116, the first year may look something like what you see on the next page.

System	2017–18 Goals
Worship	Goal 1,2,3,4,5,6
Evangelization	Goal 1,2,3
Discipleship	
Fellowship/Community	Goal 1,2,3
Ministry	

Now use the table on the next page to map your goals for three years, then create detailed plans for each of the three years on the pages that follow.

Chart Your Goals for the Next Three Years

Chart your goals that you created on the mini-plan sheets according to your mapping exercise.

System	2017–18 Goals	2018–19 Goals	2019–20 Goals
Worship			
Evangelization			
Discipleship			
Community			
Ministry			

5 · The Plan: You Need a Vision *and* a Plan

One-Year Planning Guide
Year:_____

Chart your goals that you created on the mini-plan sheets according to your mapping exercise. Under "system goals," name the system you are planning to work on and list the goals underneath.

SYSTEM GOALS	ACTION STEPS	POINT PERSONS	COMPLETION DATE	MEASUREMENT
System:_____				
System:_____				
System:_____				
System:_____				

One-Year Planning Guide
Year:_____

Chart your goals that you created on the mini-plan sheets according to your mapping exercise. Under "system goals," name the system you are planning to work on and list the goals underneath.

SYSTEM GOALS	ACTION STEPS	POINT PERSONS	COMPLETION DATE	MEASUREMENT
System:_____				
System:_____				
System:_____				
System:_____				

5 The Plan: You Need a Vision *and* a Plan

One-Year Planning Guide
Year:_____

Chart your goals that you created on the mini-plan sheets according to your mapping exercise. Under "system goals," name the system you are planning to work on and list the goals underneath.

SYSTEM GOALS	ACTION STEPS	POINT PERSONS	COMPLETION DATE	MEASUREMENT
System:_____				
System:_____				
System:_____				
System:_____				

Congratulations! You are almost there! There are still a few loose ends, but before we get into those, take a deep breath and look back at what you have created since using this guidebook. You have

- Formed a leadership team
- Adjusted your pastor's model of ministry
- Reshaped the focus of your pastoral council
- Clarified your vision and purpose
- Done a detailed assessment of your parish
- Assessed the five systems of church life and gathered the elements you need to build a five-year plan
- Dreamt about what your parish will be like in five years and created 20 mini-plans around this vision
- Organized these plans, mapped them out over five years and drilled down to create detailed plans for each year

So what's missing?

It's like anything you work on. Only when you have finished can you step back and really look at the whole thing and perhaps see what you were not able to see before.

What are you looking for? You are looking for critical success factors, gaps in your plan and barriers. Don't worry, this doesn't require a rewrite, but you do need to be aware of them.

@SaintBP

When we assembled our first five-year plan, it became evident that there were several critical factors. If we didn't get these things right, the plan would stall out. Here are the factors:

Culture: We needed to continue to slowly but intentionally shift the culture of our parish so that evangelization and discipleship were the norm.

Structure: Staff, lay leadership, ministry and governance structures had reached their maximum and could not scale to meet our projected growth. New structures and models would be required.

Leadership: New leaders to support both succession planning for existing ministries and our growth initiatives are required at all levels: staff, lay and ministries.

Communications: Clear, concise and consistent communications, both internally and externally, across multiple mediums, were required to ensure that all stakeholders were aware of our mission and plans.

Take some time on the next page to describe your critical success factors.

Critical Success Factors

What needs to happen in your parish to make your plan a success?

Related to critical success factors are specific tools and resources you may need over the next five years to successfully implement your plan. Take some time to discuss these with your leadership team.

Questions for discussion

1) What demands on human resources will be made by your plan? What staffing positions will your plan make necessary? What skills and competencies will your existing staff and leaders have to learn? Do some staff need to transition into other roles?

2) What will the financial needs of the parish be if this plan is to be successful? What will your operating budget be for the next number of years?

3) Are new systems or system changes required to meet your objectives (example: a parish database)?

4) Do processes need to be developed or changed to meet your objectives?

5) What of your assumptions must be validated to confirm that this is an achievable plan?

Conclusion

Your plan now exists within the pages of this guidebook. Perhaps a member of your pastoral council can transcribe your work into a stand-alone document.

As Steve Jobs used to say, "There's one more thing."

The point of a plan is to actually execute it. The plan will present many blessings and struggles over the next five years. There is no playbook for execution. Well, there could be, but it would be about 10 times as long as this guidebook.

You started this process with vision. Someone once said that "vision without execution is hallucination."

You didn't go through all this work to simply have a detailed map towards a distant future that sits in a drawer. As the old Nike commercial used to say, "Just do it!"

Speaking of Nike, remember that shoe store and those new shoes? Go get them!

Read about some principles for execution on pages 272–279.

6

The Weekend: The Centrality of the Eucharist

Welcome to Chapter 6! Chances are, if you are following the advice laid out in Chapter 3, you're reading this just as you are beginning work with your pastoral council on strategic planning. Strategic plans take time, and the process in chapters 3 and 4 takes over a year to complete.

Meanwhile, life goes on. The life of the parish goes on and the urgent need to start making changes goes on, too.

Here's the thing: you don't need to wait until you finish a five-year strategic plan to know that your best initial investment is in improving the weekend experience.

Chapter 5 of *Divine Renovation* is structured around 10 values that, if truly lived, will bring health to your parish. Health is key because healthy things grow and bear fruit. The first four of these values are centred on the weekend experience.

Your pastoral council has its hands full working on the big strategic plan for the parish. You, as the pastor and leadership team, will be part of that process, and you will eventually address the weekend experience under the system of worship. For now, I invite you to begin to examine how you can immediately begin to raise the bar on the weekend experience. If you have not already done so, I encourage you and your team to complete the first four of the Ten Values Analysis exercise on pages 74–75.

Let's begin by reminding ourselves why this is essential.

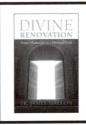

Read about giving priority to the weekend experience on pages 95–101.

Go to divinerenovation.net. Under Media, go to Exploring themes and watch the fourth video, entitled "The Importance of Culture," until the 11-minute mark.

Before we get into the three H's – hymns, homilies and hospitality – let's take a moment to examine your weekend structure.

In Chapter 4, I invited you to take a close look at the weekend Mass schedule for your parish in the context of communicating vision. The weekend homily is the single greatest tool a pastor has to win parishioners over to a particular direction. If your Mass schedule is such that the pastor cannot preach at every Mass, you will be seriously hindered in your attempts to lead your parish from maintenance to mission.

Perhaps you have already discussed this and have even completed the exercise around your Mass schedule. If you have not, don't worry, you can now kill two birds with one stone.

The goal of the exercise in Chapter 3 was to find the best Mass schedule that would allow your pastor to preach at every single Mass. The goal for this exercise was to honestly ask yourselves what Mass schedule would be the best to facilitate renewal, rather than keeping the maximum number of people happy.

A while back, I spoke to a parish in the United States that was composed of three church buildings, each about a mile away from one another. The parish had six Masses per weekend and had to use retired priests to help, as several Masses were scheduled at the same time. The irony was that the total attendance on a weekend was about 1,000 people. Do the math.

So often the Eucharist, which is meant to be about gathering our people together, is more about scattering them. In addition, think of all the time and energy wasted in providing liturgical ministries and music to all these underattended Masses. Some of the church buildings of this parish could seat 800 people; they were offering unnecessary Masses for 150 people or fewer at some of them.

The irony was that the pastor was a gifted preacher, and the Masses where *he* consistently presided and preached were growing. The money this parish was spending to keep these buildings open was astronomical.

In spite of these obvious drains on the effectiveness of the weekend experience, and on overall effectiveness, when I spoke to the pastor and his team they were highly resistant to changing anything. On the one hand, they told me that they were very serious about renewal, and on the other hand, they loved their Mass schedule. They wanted change but did not want to change.

What about you? Do you really want the change? Are you ready to change?

Let's go back to the parish I spoke about. Imagine if they reduced the number of Masses to two and closed two of their buildings.

- They could gather all their parishioners at two Masses and still be less than 70% full.
- The energy difference just from not worshipping in an empty church would have a huge impact on parishioners and visitors.
- They could focus their best liturgical ministers and musical resources to make the weekend experience amazing.
- The pastor could preach visioning homilies every three weeks and speak to all his parishioners.
- The pastor would see all his parishioners every week and they would see him.
- There would be sufficient time between Masses for parishioners to gather and for community building and faith formation events to take place.
- Millions of dollars in heating and maintenance would be saved over 10 years by moving to one building.
- The money saved could be invested in hiring staff to lead evangelization and discipleship.

The tragedy of this parish is that there are parishes like it all over North America and Europe. Pastors and pastoral councils are held hostage by the fear of upsetting a few parishioners. In the face of the overwhelming reasons to make such a change, such resistance can only be understood as a complete misunderstanding of what the Church is all about, or the selfishness of some parishioners.

What about you? Would you allow a few dozen irate parishioners to prevent you from moving forward with something like this?

Questions for discussion

1) How does your situation resemble what I have described above?

2) Does your infrastructure maximize the weekend experience, or detract from it?

3) If no parishioners were to get upset about the changes, what would your weekend schedule look like?

Let's look at the exercise that you may or may not have completed in chapter 4 on page 63 from this *different* perspective. If you completed it, just fill in the numbers in the chart below. Remember to count attendance, rather than guessing.

As I mentioned earlier, church growth experts tell us that psychologically, a church is experienced to be full when it is at 80% capacity.

With this in mind, and all the other factors involved in your particular context, what would be the optimal weekend Mass schedule for your parish? Fill out the chart below and then write down your desired schedule on the next page.

Mass Time	Seating Capacity	Average Attendance	Percentage Full

Desired Mass Schedule

You will need a plan to communicate this change. Use the next page to help you with that. You may want to visit the section on dealing with pushback in Chapter 4. Discuss the resistance and arguments that you will encounter and use the space below to write down responses that your team will use:

Mass Schedule Communication Plan

Goals	Action Steps	Point Person	Completion Date	Measurement

If we do nothing else in the next 6 months, we must:	The single most important thing we must do in the next month is:

The three H's: Hymns, homilies and hospitality

The first H: Hymns

Read the section entitled "Uplifting Music" on pages 110–122.

The first task is to look more closely at the music in your parish and to begin to discuss what may be possible.

Here are a few questions to guide your research and discussion:

1) Which are your most highly attended Masses?

2) Do you have contemporary music at any of your Masses?

3) If you could introduce contemporary music at just one Mass, which Mass time would you choose?

4) Do you have traditional sacred music at any of your Masses?

5) If you could introduce traditional sacred music at just one Mass, which Mass time would you choose?

6) How much did your parish spend on music last year? What will it spend next year, and the year after that?

7) How many paid staffing positions do you have to support music and audiovisual technology on the weekend?

8) As you add up these positions, what is their full-time equivalent?

9) Do you have screens in your church? If yes, how are they working?

10) Where could you install screens and projectors if you do not presently have any?

11) How old is your sound system?

12) Can your sound system handle contemporary music?

13) How are the acoustics in your church building? Are they optimized for the spoken word and for music of different genres?

@SaintBP

When I first arrived at Saint Benedict Parish, improving the music was one of my top priorities. We had a talented quarter-time music/choir director who was also a full-time student. That was it. We had what I would consider a typical array of parish music that was neither traditional nor contemporary, and most of the hymns that were sung were not hymns of praise. We spent most of our time singing hymns in which we talked to one another.

Presently, we have a half-time music and AV director, two quarter-time choir directors and two stipend choir directors, and several stipend cantors and section leaders of our main choir. All of these positions add up to a little more than a full-time position.

At our Saturday afternoon Mass, we have a rotation of volunteer organists and cantors. At our Sunday 9 a.m. Mass, we have our contemporary band. All the band members are non-paid parishioners. Our 11:15 a.m. Mass features a choir that does choral music, sacred polyphony and Gregorian Chant. Our 6 p.m. Mass has a large contemporary choir. We also have a funeral choir and a children's choir.

All of this has been able to happen by investing in the equivalent of a full-time position in music.

The Hymn of Praise

On pages 114–116 of *Divine Renovation*, I make a case for the primacy of the hymn of praise. In this section, I ask readers to reflect on who is being spoken to in the majority of hymns on a typical weekend.

On this page and the next one is an exercise to help you analyze the mix of genres of liturgical hymns at your weekend Masses.

Ask your music director to gather the information for you.

1) Write down your Mass times.
2) Under Hymns, there is room for as many as five hymns per Mass. Write down the names of the hymns from one particular weekend.
3) Next, identify the genre of hymn: *praise*, *petition* (speaking directly to God), *confessional* (speaking about God), *scripture* (speaking as God), *exhortation* (speaking to one another).
4) Identify the total number of hymns of praise in each Mass and your total for that weekend.

132

Date: _____

Mass Time	Hymns	Genre	# of hymns of Praise
	1. 2. 3. 4. 5.		
	1. 2. 3. 4. 5.		
	1. 2. 3. 4. 5.		
	1. 2. 3. 4. 5.		
	1. 2. 3. 4. 5.		

Mass Time	Hymns	Genre	# of hymns of Praise
	1. 2. 3. 4. 5.		
	1. 2. 3. 4. 5.		
	1. 2. 3. 4. 5.		

Total Hymns of Praise: : _____

Questions for discussion

1) What is the dominant genre of music, regardless of whether your music is in a contemporary or traditional style?

2) How can you move towards giving priority to hymns of praise?

3) What did you learn from this exercise?

4) What do you need to start doing?

5) What do you need to stop doing?

I know that planning music will eventually be in your five-year plan, under the system of worship. However, you cannot and should not wait for that plan to be completed before you begin to work on this essential element of your weekend experience. The direction of better is always a sure thing.

Use the six-month planning sheet on the next page to shape a plan based on the discussions and work you have done with your leadership team.

Music

Goals	Action Steps	Point Person	Completion Date	Measurement

If we do nothing else in the next 6 months, we must:	The single most important thing we must do in the next month is:

The second H: Homilies

 Read the section entitled "Homilies" on pages 123–135.

We spoke earlier about the need to have a Mass schedule that allows the pastor to preach at all Masses. This is an essential element of communicating vision: if you are going to change things, you need to be able to tell people the why and not just the what.

Why stop there?

If the pastor can preach at all the Masses, so can the other clergy in your parish, if you have any.

 @SaintBP

At Saint Benedict Parish, we currently have two priests, two deacons and another priest on a six-month internship. Whoever preaches on any given weekend preaches at all four Masses. This allows a consistent message to be given at every Mass on any given weekend. It also frees up the preacher to put much more time into preparing the homily, as he is likely not preaching every weekend. As pastor, I still do 40–50% of the preaching.

On Sundays, instead of celebrating or concelebrating all three Masses (technically not allowed), the priest who preaches and is not the presider will participate in the entire first part of the liturgy and then quietly leave the sanctuary after the homily, during the Creed. I know that this might drive some liturgical purists crazy, but it does allow us to have consistent, planned, focused preaching each week. This makes a difference.

There is no silver bullet when it comes to improved preaching, but the starting point is to know that no matter how gifted a pastor, associate pastor or deacon may be, he can always be better.

Here are a few suggestions. Take some time to discuss with your leadership team what it would be like to actually do it:

1) Record your homilies, preferably by video. Watch yourself and critique yourself.
2) Commit to one homily and one preacher for all Masses at your parish.
3) Enrol in a speaker training course, such as Toastmasters or Christopher Leadership Course.
4) Use slides in your homily. Keep them simple: don't overload them with too many words.
5) Invite real-time feedback on your homily, especially after the first time you give it. Find someone who will speak honestly to you and not just say, "Nice homily, Father." Adjust as necessary.
6) Take time to speak about the homily of the past weekend and the homily for the upcoming weekend at your weekly leadership team meeting.
7) If you have a gathering of clergy in your parish, take time to discuss the preaching each week.
8) During the week, have one of your teams lay on hands and pray over the preacher for God's anointing.
9) Make a decision to start doing lectionary-based preaching series if you have not already

done so. Plan one, do it and evaluate. Plan others.

10) Anticipate your preaching series at least six months in advance.
11) Bring other team members into the planning and content creation process so it truly is a team exercise.
12) Create graphics for your preaching series and advertise them.

All of these things are truly possible, because we have done all of them over the last five years at Saint Benedict Parish. We have at least doubled, if not tripled, the time and energy we put into preaching, and I think it shows.

Our friends and colleagues at the Church of the Nativity in Timonium, Maryland, have become masters of this approach.

 If you have not already done so, plan to make time to read all the publications of Fr. Michael White and Tom Corcoran. Especially on the ministry of preaching and the responsibility to give it our best efforts, I highly recommend their book *Rebuilding Your Message*.

Fr. Michael and his gifted team have been developing preaching series for years. They have created a wealth of resources – not just for each preaching series, but also ancillary resources to connect the homily themes to kids' ministry and small groups in the parish. They have made these resources available along with access to webinars and podcasts through the Rebuilt Parish Association. It's great stuff. Saint Benedict Parish is a member. Visit rebuiltparishassociation.com and sign up your parish.

 @SaintBP

We first started to do preaching series at Saint Benedict Parish around our three annual stewardship initiatives, which focused on a call to discipleship, ministry and financial giving. At the time, aside from the times I would preach a visioning homily at all the Masses, each preacher prepared his own homily based on agreed key points and asks. It never really worked well.

It also meant that, no matter what, I was always preaching every single weekend. To be honest, I'm not sure why it took me so long to change what we were doing.

We started having one preacher for every weekend in my third year as pastor. We started having back-to-back preaching series at the beginning of my fifth year as pastor. Themes, graphics, outlines of each week, key points and specific asks are all identified months in advance. One of our staff members (not a priest) does the advance work with the lectionary. Possible themes are discussed at our leadership team meetings and eventually a preaching document is prepared for each series that is focused, rich and fluid enough to allow for the creativity and style of each preacher.

On the next page you will find a simple preaching guide we use at Saint Benedict Parish. This brief form captures the main elements spoken about in *Divine Renovation*. We ask our preachers to complete this form before they begin to write or build their homily. Perhaps it will be of some use in your parish.

Preaching Guide

Homilist: _____

Weekend: _____

Readings:

Scriptural Theme:

What I want people to know:

What I want people to do:

Why does it matter:

Content Check

_____ Hook?

_____ Humour Point?

_____ Personal Element?

_____ Kerygma?

_____ Does it feel like Good News?

So how will preaching be different in your parish six months from now? We have highlighted many ideas and resources in this section on preaching. Which will you use?

Take some time to discuss this with your leadership team and set three goals for you to achieve in the next six months. Use the planning sheet on the next page to help you organize your thoughts and develop a plan.

6-Month Planning Guide

Homilies

Goals	Action Steps	Point Person	Completion Date	Measurement

If we do nothing else in the next 6 months, we must:	The single most important thing we must do in the next month is:

The Weekend: The Centrality of the Eucharist

The third H: Hospitality

Read the section entitled "Hospitality" on pages 101–110.

As mentioned in *Divine Renovation*, the goal of hospitality is not just to maximize the pleasantness of a visit to church, but to maximize that potential for this visit to be the first of a series of steps towards becoming missionary disciples.

Questions for discussion

1) Do you have a clearly defined process to bring people from attending church for the first time to becoming missionary disciples?

2) If you have a process, how well does your leadership team, staff, ministry leaders and hospitality ministers know it?

3) How effective is your process to bring people from attending to being an active part of your community?

4) On a scale of 1 to 10, how would you score the effectiveness of this process?

5) How are people with a non-Church background or non-Catholics brought into this process?

Remember, as per the basic theme of *Divine Renovation*, the goal of this process is not just to be friendly or help someone register for the parish, but to help them take their first steps on the journey towards becoming a missionary disciple. If belonging does lead to believing, which in turn leads to behaving, the immediate goal is to bring people into an experience of belonging as soon as possible. Belonging, however, is not an end in itself. The ultimate goal is to make disciples and then to make disciples become apostles.

On the next page, describe your ideal version of an assimilation or welcoming process to bring people from the front door into the heart of your community. Name each specific step, beginning with the first time someone attends, and describe the objectives of each step. If it takes more than five steps (including walking through your door) to be drawn into the life of your parish, your process is too complicated.

When you have completed this, use the six-month planning guide on page 142 to make a plan to implement and communicate your process.

New Parishioners Welcoming Process

STEP	OBJECTIVES

Welcoming Process

Goals	Action Steps	Point Person	Completion Date	Measurement

If we do nothing else in the next 6 months, we must:	**The single most important thing we must do in the next month is:**

Through the eyes of a stranger

Some of the things we are the most blind to are the most familiar.

A number of years back, our music director at the time was having a conversation with a staff member from another parish about screens and projectors in the church. This person was resistant to the idea of there being such things in *her* church. When the music director mentioned that we put the responses to the prayers of the Mass on the screens, she said, "At our parish we presume that *our* parishioners know the parts of the Mass." Our music director replied, "At Saint Benedict, we presume that there are new people present who do not know the parts of the Mass."

So what is presumed at your parish? We all make presumptions, often without knowing we are making them. That's the problem with presuming. Look at the weekend experience at your parish. What presumptions are built into the experience?

Take some time on the next page to write down as many presumptions as you can think of. They can be good or bad. They can be wise or foolish. They can be true or false. Just write down what you presume; don't filter them. It will be a mixed bag, but it is a bag full of things that shape what you do on any given weekend.

If this exercise is too difficult to do, invite a non-parishioner, a fallen-away Catholic, a non-Catholic Christian and a non-Christian to come to your church and report back to you what it was like.

Presumptions
Part 1

Brainstorm below about the presumptions that are built into what you do on the weekend and how you do it. Don't filter: if they are operative, write them down.

Presumptions
Part 2

Now classify your presumptions in the chart below.

TRUE	FALSE

WISE	FOOLISH

GOOD	BAD

Presumptions
Part 3

From your list of false, foolish and bad presumptions, write down below how these presumptions have impacted the experience of someone new to your parish, or to the world of the Church. Be specific. What habits and practices have these presumptions led to?

@SaintBP

"Pointers for Pastoral Presiding," December 31, 2015 – by Fr. Simon Lobo, C.C.

At Christmas, we had well over 3,000 people through the building at a total of five celebrations. This included our non-liturgical *Christmas Unplugged* service, which had about 120 guests and 15 staff/volunteers. FJM dressed up as St. Nick at the latter, and read a children's Christmas story. Unfortunately, he had a wardrobe malfunction (with his beard) and was exposed by one of the girls as a "Fake Santa".

All in all, our efforts of our preaching series *Getting Ready for Company*, which ran during the four Sundays of Advent, were well received. Here are a few other things we incorporated this year. Before each of the Masses, we had one or two staff members give a welcome message, which was followed by a short video to set the tone for Christmas Mass. We also put *Why Jesus?* booklets in the pews (an Alpha resource). Many flipped through them as they were waiting for Mass to begin. We invited our guests to take a copy home with them. As with any liturgy where a lot of non-practising folks are expected, FJM added a few explanations to give guidance at key moments. These are a few paraphrases of the main messages:

Greeting (before the Penitential Rite): We have a local custom at SBP in that we want everyone to have a "prayer partner". Don't worry – it's not difficult. It helps us to enter into Mass as a community together. We want to make sure that each person here has someone else praying for him or her. Turn to a person near you, introduce yourself, and agree to pray for them. Later (at the end of the Prayer of the Faithful), we will have an opportunity to offer a silent prayer, in our hearts, for that person.

Sign of Peace: As we are about to offer one another a sign of peace, let's remember that this gesture is, in a sense, a prayer. "I pray that you know peace in your life"… the kind of peace that Jesus brings to us in a special way at Christmastime.

Communion: For the sake of visitors from outside of our tradition… in a few moments we will have the opportunity to share in the Sacrament of the Body and Blood of Jesus. It represents union with Jesus, but it is also a "public declaration of being an active member of the Catholic Church." We want to respect everyone, and we don't want for anyone to make that kind of statement if it is not true. We want you to be true to yourself. If you are in a place where you are not able to receive Holy Communion, you are welcome to come forward. We simply ask that you cross your arms over your chest, and we will be happy to pray a blessing over you.

(I was shocked to see the number of people who came forward with arms crossed and with smiles on their faces. I think they felt free to not have to pretend.)

Leaving Early (could be added to the previous announcement): This is a very special time of prayer. Please don't leave. It's not over until it's over. We've still got a lot of praying to do. We'll get home (the turkey is still half-frozen, the gifts are still going to be there). Just stay and be with Jesus, and let's take a moment of prayer together.

> (I was amazed by how few *Judases* we had – people who leave the supper early.)
>
> *What do I want you to know?*
>
> At SBP, we presume that there will be guests in our midst, especially during Christmas. As a result, we went out of our way to make the typically "outsider unfriendly" liturgy as warm and understandable as possible.
>
> In the past, I have often been annoyed with the unchurched who did not know what to do or say. It has been a good exercise for me to look inwards first and ask, "What am I doing to set our guests up for success?" The fruit is that many commented on how they felt really welcome and some even said that they plan on coming back.
>
> *What do I want you to do?*
>
> Discuss, with your liturgy team, which of these messages and tactics would be appropriate for your own context. Be attentive to the high-traffic seasons when you anticipate having a lot of people who are unfamiliar with the Mass. Consider adding one of these messages at the next available opportunity and evaluate how it goes.
>
> I realize that liturgy and presidential styles can be sensitive topics. In no way am I suggesting that this is the way to go or that implementing a few of these blurbs will save the day. These explanations are part of a much broader approach – to create an "invitational culture" – that continues to be a work in progress.

As mentioned in *Divine Renovation*, I believe that the liturgy is inherently inhospitable. It presumes so much that is not true for many people who come to Mass every week, and certainly not true for the unchurched who occasionally show up.

The liturgy is meant for the evangelized and the committed. It presumes this. It seeks to feed disciples and send them out to be missionary disciples in the world.

In addition to this, our Catholic tradition is a liturgical tradition. We are not free as other Christian churches are to create something new from the ground up in order to be "seeker sensitive." The liturgy is not seeker sensitive. This is why, at Saint Benedict Parish, our primary interface with the unchurched is not the weekend, but Alpha. We will be talking about this more in the next chapter.

Nevertheless, unless we are going to put up signs on our churches that say that the Eucharist is only for committed Catholics who have become missionary disciples, there will always be unevangelized, uncommitted, non-Catholic, non-Christian, untidy, unfamiliar, unknowledgable people at Mass. Therefore, we are obliged to make the celebration of the Eucharist as hospitable as we can.

The point is that if we go through a weekend presuming that no one from the outside is there, eventually no one from the outside will be there, because they will never come back.

We can do lots of things around the Sunday experience to achieve this that are not strictly liturgical, but I believe that we must squeeze the Sunday liturgy a little bit for the sake of those who are unknown and unknowing. I say "a little," because if we squeeze too much we will not respect the integrity of the liturgy. There is a point beyond which our worship will no longer be Catholic.

On the next page, take some time to brainstorm ideas of how you can make the entire Sunday experience, liturgical and non-liturgical, more welcoming, hospitable and accessible to those on the outside.

When you have finished this task, choose three actions and create a plan to implement and communicate the changes.

Operation Accessibility

Brainstorm ideas of how you can make the entire Sunday experience, liturgical and non-liturgical, more welcoming, hospitable and accessible to those on the outside. Write down your ideas below.

6-Month Planning Guide

Operation Accessibility

Goals	Action Steps	Point Person	Completion Date	Measurement

If we do nothing else in the next 6 months, we must:

The single most important thing we must do in the next month is:

Conclusion

Investing in your weekend experience is the biggest bang for your buck. If you get this right, your attendance will go up, your collection will go up and parishioners will be much more likely to invite others to join them for Mass, because they will have confidence that it will always be an amazing experience.

Even more than this, you will have a powerful means to share the vision with parishioners, to win them and inspire them. Your increase in resources, both human and material, will give you what you need to continue on the path from maintenance to mission.

But there's still more to do, because more butts in pews and more money in the collection is not the end game.

The Processes: Replace Programs with Process

I've never been much of a one for sailing, but since I live by the Atlantic Ocean and can see it from my window, I can only imagine what it would be like to do a trans-Atlantic sailing trip.

Years ago I heard Bill Hybels speak about the three stages of a journey and how this applies to implementing a vision. Since that time, I have used the metaphor of a trans-Atlantic voyage for the journey of leading a church from maintenance to mission. The three stages are obvious: the beginning, the middle and the end.

Phase 1 of the journey of parish renewal begins when you begin to execute your plan. It is in execution that the ship begins to move. I am sure that by the time you have reached this chapter, although your planning continues, you have already started to execute, to move your ship.

In the world of parish renewal, for most Catholic parishes there is the necessity of overcoming a crippling inertia. This is rooted in the fact that evangelization and discipleship are so often not the norm in parishes. They are not part of the culture. In the Catholic Church, evangelization and discipleship has for decades been the work of so many ecclesial movements. Catholics who came alive in their faith were often forced to find the essentials of the Christian life outside of their parishes, and would only return to their parishes to receive the sacraments – and, to be honest, were usually considered to be a bit odd by other parishioners.

This dynamic has haunted me since I came alive in my faith at the age of 18. It has bothered me throughout the years. Since that time I wondered why the experiences I had with a group of young committed Catholics on Tuesday nights at a Cursillo gathering could not be incorporated into the life of a parish. These experiences of Christian life seemed to run parallel to each other and only crossed over at the celebration of the Eucharist. The desire to close this gap is what has driven me as a pastor since the year 2000.

What must be done to normalize the abnormal in our parishes? Lots of hard, persistent work. The only way to make evangelization normal is to do evangelization – not just talk about it, but do it and celebrate it when lives are transformed by the Lord Jesus.

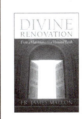

I really, really encourage you to read the section entitled "How to Transform the Culture of the Parish Community" on pages 87–95. It will frame up all the exercises in this chapter.

@SaintBP

Normalizing what isn't normal is rather… abnormal. Certainly it feels that way when you begin. There will be pushback. Some people get uncomfortable; you may receive a few complaints and anonymous letters. The great thing is that the second time you do it it's easier, and so on.

The greatest tool we used at Saint Benedict Parish to begin to change the culture was Alpha. I describe Alpha to a great extent in *Divine Renovation*, so there's no need to repeat that here. As soon as we finished our first run of Alpha, there were so many stories of changed lives that it was hard to choose which ones to share, but choose we did.

Since that time, frequent lay testimonies after the homily about how people have encountered Jesus in a life-changing way have become normal at our parish. Prayer breakfasts that feature "normal" people telling their stories of encounter with Jesus slowly become the norm. Our monthly newsletters and even our annual finance report feature stories of changed lives. We do this because that's what it's all about: changed lives!

As I write these words, about 60% of our parishioners have done Alpha over the last five years. We intentionally did not seek to put all our parishioners through at once, because cultural change takes time. During that time, many unchurched, fallen away and non-believers came through Alpha, experienced a conversion and are now full members of the Church and are leading ministry.

It simply has become… normal.

The Process of Changing the Culture

The central task of leadership for the sake of the renewal of the Church *is* the task of leading cultural change.

This is an essential point to grasp.

So far in this guidebook, we have spoken about getting the right people on your leadership team and forming the right plan. Soon we will speak about the right process, the right people and even the place of programs. None of these things will ultimately matter, however, if the culture of the parish is not transformed.

The business management leader Peter Drucker used to say that "culture eats strategy for breakfast."

In the world of the local Church, culture will eat P's for breakfast:

- **P**eople
- **P**lans
- **P**rocesses
- **P**rograms

What does this mean for us?

First, it will take time. Parish renewal is not a sprint, but a marathon. Real change is possible, but it takes time. Changing the P's – the people, plans, processes and programs – without changing the culture will simply not bear fruit. Cultural change takes place when the members of a church not only cannot go back, but do not want to go back.

@SaintBP

During the first three years at Saint Benedict Parish, we used Alpha and an annual series of Stewardship initiatives focused on discipleship, ministry and financial giving. We ran Alpha and countless faith formation programs and reached the point of 40% involvement. We had ministry fairs and commitment Sundays to call parishioners to step up and serve, and addressed financial giving through preaching and testimonies and called parishioners to commit to their giving. All these things were far from normal at first. In repeating them over and over again, we slowly saw a transformation in what was considered to be normal.

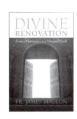

Read more about some of the things we did to begin to shift the culture of our parish in the early years at Saint Benedict Parish in the section entitled "Clear Expectations," on pages 153–164.

Let's go back to that sailing analogy and that trans-Atlantic trip.

Phase 1 of the journey will end when you can no longer see the shore from which you left. As Winston Churchill famously said in a 1942 speech, just after the British drove German troops out of Egypt, "Now, this is not the end. It is not even the beginning of the end. But it is, perhaps, the end of the beginning." The end of the beginning will be with you sooner than later. At the parishes I have led through this first phase of renewal, it took, on average, four years to gain momentum on this cultural transformation.

Phase 2 of the journey is when you can see neither the shore from which you left nor the shore to which you are going. This is the scariest and riskiest part of the journey. It is in the middle that doubts arise and mutinies take place. If the goal of phase 1 was to gain momentum on creating a culture of evangelization and discipleship, phase 2 is about focus, alignment and systems.

Think of it like this. We get a lot of snow where I live (in the winter). When a car is stuck in the snow, it takes a lot of energy and force to get it moving. You have to rock it back and forth, and push and push and push. Once it starts moving, you don't have to push hard anymore, just gently. The driver also must begin to steer the car.

This is like the phases of parish renewal. If your parish is stuck in the snow of maintenance culture, you need to push, push and push. You need to rock it back and forth. This is what we did with Alpha, testimonies, stewardship initiatives, programs, programs and programs. But once the car broke loose and began to move, we had to shift gears and begin to do things differently.

This is phase 2: it requires a light push and a tight hand on the steering wheel. It was at this point that we had to change our model of discipleship. We had outgrown our building, so we had to start pushing the gatherings into homes. More importantly, we had to move from discipleship being about programs to being about process – the process of making missionary disciples.

Our goal now is to say no to as many new things as possible to reduce the amount of sideways energy that can distract us from the main thing of forming disciples who joyfully live out the mission of Jesus Christ. We have adopted the mantra of "less is more," because it is more effective to do fewer things with excellence than to do many things reasonably well.

Phase 3 begins when your destination is in sight. What is that destination? It is when a parish is living as a missionary parish, when your daily reality closely reflects what you have described in your parish vision statement. You are still far from perfect and still deal with problems, but the fruits of your labours are all around you.

This chapter is entitled "The Processes" because we are speaking of two different processes: the process of the transformation of the culture of a parish, and a process for forming missionary disciples. These two processes, however, are intertwined, because every time someone becomes a missionary disciple, your parish will be one step closer to truly being a missionary parish. Being a truly missionary parish does not happen through establishing ministries and structures. It will happen when the number of missionary disciples in your parish reaches a critical mass and, without your even noticing when you crossed over, you will experience yourself in a truly missionary parish.

So let's get to work.

I have proposed that the journey to complete cultural transformation (that is, the journey from maintenance to mission) is composed of three distinct phases. The process of cultural change takes time: I propose that each phase takes about four years. Below is a schema that outlines the main goals and needs of each phase.

Phase 1	Phase 2	Phase 3
Goal:	Goal:	Goal:
Creating momentum towards establishing a culture of evangelization and discipleship	Creating systems, alignment, focus & clarity. Moving from programs to process	Growth. Equipping disciples for ministry. Outward-focused Church. Change the world!
Needs:	Needs:	Needs:
Evangelization, testimonies, clear expectations, faith formation opportunities, centralized model, repetition	Decentralized model, restructured staff, doing fewer things, saying no. Clearly defined discipleship process.	Keep the discipleship process the main thing. Get out of the way.
Four Years	Four Years	Four Years

Now, anyone could argue that this is simply a theory, and that person would be correct, strictly speaking.

In my years as a pastor, I have brought three different parishes through the first phase of renewal. It took about four years each time. Until Saint Benedict Parish, however, I had never directly experienced the second phase, as I was always moved to another parish before that point. In my opinion, as I write these words, we are presently about halfway through this second phase (after six years). There have been many challenges, discoveries and learnings in this new phase, and I have had to adapt my leadership once again. So, about those last four years of phase 3… ask me in 2022 if I was right.

Some may contend that this first phase is not necessary. In my experience it is, if you find yourself leading a typical Catholic parish that has no culture of evangelization and discipleship. Again, it's not necessarily that no one is doing these things in the parish, but it is a small minority of parishioners who are living as missionary disciples.

In such a parish, if a pastor immediately decentralized, and created systems and focus, everything would collapse: no one would engage the systems and the focus would alienate almost all the parishioners and tear the parish apart. I've seen it happen.

As you are reading these pages, you have obviously begun your journey and may have been on it for many years now. Discuss with your leadership team where you are on the journey from maintenance to mission and mark your spot with an x on the arrow.

Phase 1	Phase 2	Phase 3
←—————————————————————————————————→		
Years:	Years:	Years:

@SaintBP

By the end of my third year at Saint Benedict Parish, it was clear that things were really beginning to change. As exciting as the move towards evangelization and discipleship was, it created its own set of problems. The multiplication of programs and the fact that they were all organized by parish staff and held in the building brought us to a breaking point. If we kept going the way we were going, it would blow up in our faces. I was at the point of exhaustion, and so were the staff, the ministry leaders and the building.

Someone once said that the most difficult model to change is a model that is working. Ours was working, but the very fact that it *had* worked so well meant that it was no longer working so well.

We stopped doing stewardship initiatives. We put new ministries on hold and encouraged those that were not sustainable to close down. We made a move towards one primary process for making missionary disciples and embraced the philosophy of "Less is More." We immediately found that it was true. More is not merrier, and we actually accomplished more for the Kingdom of God by focusing on fewer things.

A few years ago, I did a Google search and found an old photograph of a race car driver named Les Moore. We printed off the photo, framed it and hung it in the room where our leadership team meets. I tell you that his eyes follow you around the room and bore into anyone proposing that we take on another new project.

Questions for discussion with your leadership team

Even if you are not yet at phase 2 of renewal, take some time to discuss these questions. It will not be time wasted.

1) What do you have to start saying no to?

2) How much of your time and energy goes into dealing with requests from outside groups and ministries?

3) How much of your time and energy goes into dealing with ministry ideas from your own parishioners (both good ideas and bad ideas)?

4) How often do you give up your "pulpit" on a weekend to travelling preachers who come among you with their own version of the main thing?

5) What ministries have you been propping up but need to let die?

6) What ministries do you have to help die?

7) What models of ministry have stopped working?

REDUCE, REDUCE, REDUCE

In most of our churches, the presumption is that we will automatically do in the coming year everything we did in the previous year. If we add anything new, we do this too, in addition to everything else we did. As you look ahead at the coming ministry season, what are some things you can stop doing? Use your one-sentence purpose statement to narrow the focus, and write below the things you need to stop doing.

The process of making missionary disciples

This is the second process, and it is ultimately the key to the first process. A Church becomes a church of disciples ready to go on mission when it actually becomes a church that *makes* disciples ready to go on mission. I know this sounds obvious, but it really is as simple as that.

We spoke in the last exercise of the things you need to stop doing. You need to stop doing them not to ease up the workload, but to invest in what actually works, in what actually fulfills your purpose, as Pope Francis likes to say, of making missionary disciples.

The key question as you look at evangelization and discipleship in your parish – if you are now entering phase 2 of your journey – is how does it all fit together? How do we move from a menu of options to a simplified process with clear elements?

Think of your experience of eating in restaurants. Usually, the better the food, the thinner the menu.

Once you have momentum in creating a culture of evangelization and discipleship, the next task is to simplify and change your model. You need to move from a menu of programs to a simple process.

Before we go further on this question, let's stop for a moment.

In Chapter 5, when speaking of the five systems, we spoke about the essential task of defining our terms. Today in the Church it is very trendy to speak about evangelization, and everything we do ends up being called evangelization. In my experience, where everything is evangelization, usually nothing is evangelization.

It is a similar thing to making missionary disciples, or whatever you choose to call the thing Jesus told us we are supposed to make.

We are about to invite you to reflect on and design a process for making missionary disciples, but have you actually stopped to define and agree upon what missionary disciples look like in your context? What is the finished product? No manufacturer would design a factory without knowing what the finished product should look like.

 @SaintBP

About three years into my tenure at Saint Benedict Parish, we began to speak about our need to move from programs to an intentional process for making missionary disciples.

At one particular meeting, one of our staff members, Tanya Rodgerson, asked an obvious question that all of us had missed.

"What does one actually look like?"

We sat there feeling rather silly. We all had our own ideas of what a parishioner who was living as a missionary disciple actually looked like, but we had never sat down and agreed upon a common description.

Here's what we came up with:

- Has a personal relationship with Jesus
- Can and does share faith with others
- Is open to the gifts of the Holy Spirit
- Has knowledge and love of the Scriptures
- Knows basic Catholic theology
- Has a daily prayer life
- Experiences real Christian community
- Has a commitment to Sunday Eucharist
- Celebrates the Sacrament of Reconciliation
- Can pray spontaneously out loud when asked
- Serves in ministry
- Sees his or her life as a mission field

No description of what a missionary disciple is going to be is exhaustive, and it certainly is not meant to be exclusive.

Several years ago, I was speaking to a group of church leaders about this. One person took offence at the suggestion that we should even attempt to define the characteristics of a missionary disciple. He seemed to have understood that I was saying that a person had to fit this description or they were not welcome in the parish. Not at all.

Let me use an analogy.

Those of you who are parents, think of when your children were toddlers. You know that caring for them in their immaturity was not in conflict with the vision you had for their maturity. Imagine a parent sitting his two-year-old down for a session of tough love:

"Look, kid, I'm sick and tired of you freeloading off your mother and me. You sit around the house all day, sleeping, playing and filling your diaper. You don't clean your own room. You're spoiled; you have no impulse control. It's time for you to get off your padded backside and go out and get a job."

It's a silly example, I know, but the fact that this conversation would never happen does not mean that parents have no desire for their child to grow and mature, get a job and be a valuable, contributing member of society. Every parent desires his or her child to grow to be mature and healthy. It is the same in the Church. The goal of pastoral care is to make disciples (evangelization) and to bring them to maturity (discipleship). There is nothing wrong with having clarity around what maturity looks like.

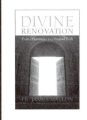 To read more about maturity as the goal of pastoral care, read the sections entitled "Redefining Pastoral Care" and "Equipping the Saints" on pages 80–84.

Let's be clear that I am most certainly not advocating intolerance against immaturity, but against a culture of immaturity. A healthy church will always have immature believers in it. If a church was ever to proudly proclaim that all its members had finally arrived at maturity, that would be a church in decline. It would have stopped having spiritual babies a long time ago. The Church is a fecund mother, teeming with life and giving birth to new spiritual babies all the time. Babies will always be immature, but babies are meant to grow up.

So, what does a mature believer look like in your parish?

Take some time with your leadership team to describe below what a missionary disciple should look like in your parish. What is the product you are trying to make, understanding that discipleship is a lifelong process and that we never stop maturing and being formed into the image of Christ? Be specific: avoid euphemisms such as "on fire" or "engaged." Name real outcomes that are measurable.

What Does a Missionary Disciple Look Like in Your Parish?

...know your need for a simple,
...disciples equipped
...what one
...ook at the

Pope Francis and the Aparecida Document on pages 35–41.

As you have read in *Divine Renovation*, Pope Francis, when he was Cardinal Bergoglio, was the lead writer of the pivotal document simply known as the Aparecida Document. The centrepiece of this document, in section 6.2.1, is the identification of "five fundamental aspects in the process of forming missionary disciples." It sounds like we don't have to reinvent the wheel. Let's look again at what he and the Latin American bishops, in union with Pope Benedict, proposed.

The "five fundamental aspects" are as follows:

1) KERYGMA: the proclamation of Jesus Christ that is "distinctly heard" and leads to "encounter with Jesus Christ."
2) CONVERSION: leads to transformed life and a decision to follow Jesus as Lord. It is actualized in the Sacrament of Baptism or Reconciliation.
3) DISCIPLESHIP: the believer constantly matures in knowledge and love of Jesus. Catechesis and Sacraments are of "fundamental importance for this stage."
4) COMMUNION: meaningful community that leads to an encounter with other disciples, a place of encouragement, support and maturation.
5) MISSION: to proclaim Jesus to others with joy, to love and serve the needy and to build the kingdom of God.

There is no question that these fundamentals of the process of making missionary disciples sound a great deal like the five systems proposed by Rick Warren that we focused on in Chapter 5 (curiously, worship is not included among the five aspects of Aparecida).

Use the chart on the next page to identify where these aspects are being lived out presently in the activities and programs of your parish.

Where and When?

Consider the five aspects and their characteristics outlined in the Aparecida Document and pinpoint when and where they currently take place within your parish. Don't be afraid to leave blanks.

ASPECT	QUALITY	RESULT	WHERE & WHEN?
KERYGMA	Clear proclamation of Jesus Christ that is "distinctly heard."	Personal encounter with Jesus Christ	
CONVERSION	Transformed life	A decision to follow Jesus. Sacrament of Baptism or Reconciliation	
DISCIPLESHIP	"Constantly matures" in the knowledge and love of Jesus	Engages sacraments and catechesis	
COMMUNION	Meaningful community where other disciples are encountered	Gives & receives encouragement, support and maturation	
MISSION	Immediate, not subsequent to discipleship	Proclaims Jesus to others with joy and serves the poor and needy.	

Questions for discussion

1) What are you doing well?

2) What are you not doing well?

3) Are there any gaps in the process?

4) How will you fill these gaps?

5) How can these aspects be connected as a process?

This last question is the k...
If you are truly in phase 2...
will have all the aspects co...
they in a process?

For your purposes, I...
adding two other elemen...
evangelization and worsh...

Pre-evangelization...
would do to prepare peo...
tion of the Gospel. The ... serving people through mi... ..ng trust and
inviting them.

Worship takes place anytime the mind and heart are raised to God in praise and thanksgiving. As Catholics, the high point of worship is the Eucharist, where we join ourselves to the eternal worship of Jesus to the Father. For us, evangelization is not complete until people are brought to the fullness of the Eucharist – the Eucharist can then truly be the source and summit of the Christian life.

@SaintBP

In years four and five of my time at Saint Benedict Parish, we moved from a model of programs to process. Over the first three years, as we witnessed long-time parishioners, fallen-away Catholics and non-Christians becoming missionary disciples, we identified the process that had emerged that was producing these results. We worked to clarify and simplify it. What emerged is what we call the GAME PLAN. It is, in effect, our strategy for making missionary disciples. It is a process, but not a linear process. God works in mysterious ways and there are many on ramps to the process. It is, however, still a process and one that embraces all the aspects outlined in the Aparecida Document. See the next page for what we came up with.

How Saint Benedict Parish forms disciples who joyfully live out the mission of Jesus Christ

THE GAME PLAN

I'd like to offer here a brief description of the elements of the Saint Benedict Parish GAME PLAN and how they relate dynamically to each other:

The starting point is the "Invitational Church" icon. This is represented by an arrow. This is not a ministry or program but a mindset or "heartset." It is an attitude, a disposition towards others. We strive to have an invitational culture at Saint Benedict Parish. This simply means that we invite. In fact, we invite so much that it is just normal. It's what we do, whether to Mass, to Alpha, a Prayer Breakfast, a concert or any of the other events we host.

The second icon is Alpha. It is easily recognizable. We have been clear that we would love all parishioners and all who wish to be a part of our parish to take Alpha. At Alpha, people hear the Gospel in a fresh way, they often encounter Jesus, experience the Holy Spirit and are welcomed into an experience of Christian community like none other. This does not mean that anyone who refuses to take Alpha is not welcome our parish, but it does mean that we will always be inviting everyone to experience more. We have found that Alpha is a the best first step for people who have been away from church or have had little to no experience of the Christian faith. The Mass presumes so much. Alpha is the best tool I have ever found; we want all of our parishioners to be familiar with this tool so they can share it with others.

The next steps are the follow-up to Alpha. We strive to have as many guests as possible go on to join a Connect Group (the circle of dots) or to come back as a member of the team for the next Alpha (the "A" arrowhead). When they are invited and then join an Alpha Team, people continue to grow spiritually, begin to serve and eventually exercise leadership. We desire Alpha team training to impact every single ministry in our parish. We always strive to have 50% first-time team members on every Alpha. This means that serving on an Alpha Team is only for a period of time, because we desire everyone to move through Alpha to another ministry and not stay in it.

The other option is to join a Connect Group. A Connect Group is a mid-sized home group of 20 to 30 people who have completed Alpha. We currently have eleven of these groups that meet every two weeks. They are lay led and are places where parishioners are known, loved and cared for in a way that could never happen if it was simply up to the priest or the parish staff. At a Connect Group, members gather for a potluck meal, a time of prayer, reflection and discussion. Amazing things happen every single week in our Connect Groups. We form new Connect Groups when we have identified, called forth and equipped new leaders.

Any parishioner can be involved in ministry. Ministry is symbolized in the GAME PLAN graphic by a heart with a dot in the middle. Our hope is that every parishioner will be involved in at least one ministry. Ideally, we seek to have ministry involvement shepherded from within a Connect Group. Connect Group leaders will encourage and check in with their members about their current ministry. We desire all parishioners in ministry to be serving from their God-given talents in a life-giving way and not just taking their turn to do their bit out of duty, guilt or obligation.

Discipleship Groups are small groups that are focused on learning content. These may be Bible Study groups or some adult faith formation programs. They are small groups of 4 to 10 people. Unlike Connect Groups, they are temporary, only meeting to do a particular program with no expectation beyond that. We encourage every parishioner, whether in a Connect Group or not, to participate in at least one Discipleship Group each year.

The final icon represents worship, especially when we gather for the Eucharist. It is our conviction that it is only when the fullness of the Christian life is being lived with some kind of involvement in these other aspects that the Eucharist has its proper place as the "source and the summit of the Christian life," as the Second Vatican Council said. When we are evangelized and in a discipleship process, seeing and experiencing community, worship, especially the Mass, will come to life.

Our invitation to parishioners is to "Get in the Game." If you want to grow in your relationship with Jesus, "Get in the Game." If you want to experience nurturing and caring, don't wait for the priest to show up at your door: "Get in the Game." If you want to experience the fullness of the Christian life and have the Eucharist truly come to life, "Get in the Game." You don't have to do everything at once. You can take one step at a time, but "Get in the Game."

You can see below how each aspect outlined in the Aparecida Document is covered by the Saint Benedict GAME PLAN:

ASPECT	QUALITY	RESULT	WHERE & WHEN?
KERYGMA	Clear proclamation of Jesus Christ that is "distinctly heard."	Personal encounter with Jesus Christ	Alpha (Mass, special events)
CONVERSION	Transformed life	A decision to follow Jesus. Sacrament of Baptism or reconciliation	Alpha
DISCIPLESHIP	"Constantly matures" in the knowledge and love of Jesus	Engages sacraments and catechesis	Discipleship Groups Alpha Team (Family Faith Formation Youth & Kids Ministry)
COMMUNION	Meaningful community where other disciples are encountered	Gives and receives encouragement, support and maturation	Connect Groups
MISSION	Immediate, not subsequent to discipleship	Proclaims Jesus to others with joy and serves the poor and needy.	Ministry Alpha (Everyday life)

Your Process for Forming Missionary Disciples

Work together as a leadership team and sketch out your process based on the elements you identified on page 160. Be careful to communicate process, but don't make it too linear.

The secret sauce

A visitor to our parish in 2016 observed that the secret sauce of our strategy to parish renewal was

1) A grounding in the human
2) Best leadership practices
3) A focus on empowerment by the Holy Spirit.

No strategy or plan to form disciples who are mission ready will be complete until these disciples have been empowered by the Holy Spirit. In the closing verses of Luke's Gospel, Jesus told his disciples to stay in Jerusalem until they were clothed with power from on high (Luke 24:49). The transition from disciples to missionary disciples (disciples who are sent) is the empowerment of the Holy Spirit.

In the end, a plan, focus, alignment, an intentional process and great communication alone will not make this happen.

Read about the importance of the experience of the Holy Spirit in the lives of disciples on pages 176–190.

In my work with parishes, there is often a desire to keep the spiritual aspect of making missionary disciples to simple, quiet personal prayer. This is absolutely necessary for living out the mission, but experiencing the power of the Holy Spirit is just as necessary to move the disciple to becoming an apostle: the same Holy Spirit who turned frightened, defeated disciples into Apostles at Pentecost. The Spirit came in power and the Church was born. If the Church is to be reborn and made new, disciples must experience the Spirit of Power in their lives. This value must truly be lived.

Go to divinerenovation.net. Under Media, go to Exploring themes and watch the fifth video, entitled "The Role of the Holy Spirit."

Almost there

Chances are that you have just clarified what you have already been doing. In a sense, you are moving as a team from unconscious competence to conscious competence.

As mentioned at the start of this chapter, the task now is to keep this main thing the main thing. You will want to work to have clarity at all levels of your parish, beginning with your parish staff, then your pastoral council, your ministry leaders and all your parishioners.

You will want to plan a sustained communication strategy with specific goals to reach every level of your parish. In mid-2015, our leadership team established a goal that in one year 60% of our parishioners would be able to draw the GAME PLAN on the back of a napkin (we stole that idea from the Ferguson Brothers at Community Church in the Chicago area).

As of the writing of this guidebook, we have started, but we're not there yet!

Why is this important? Because it's the basic plan for how we are going to fulfill our purpose. We want a majority of parishioners to help fulfill the plan, so we need them to be clear about it as well, not just the leadership.

Take some time on the next page to create a plan to communicate your own process for making missionary disciples.

6-Month Planning Guide

Missionary Disciple Formation Process Communication Plan

Goals	Action Steps	Point Person	Completion Date	Measurement

If we do nothing else in the next 6 months, we must:

The single most important thing we must do in the next month is:

@SaintBP

"Peeking at the Playbook," February 4, 2016 –
by Fr. Simon Lobo, C.C.

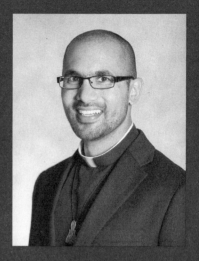

As we approach Superbowl Sunday, I am reminded of another sports analogy. Every successful football coaching staff has some kind of a playbook with all their best strategies written down with Xs and Os and arrows. I remember, growing up, going to our weekly altar boys' group on Saturday mornings. After Mass, a spiritual reflection and snacks, the lot of us went outside to play tackle football. Just like the pros, we would have a huddle, and the quarterback would draw out the play on the palm of his hand. Usually speed and brawn won the day. But every once in a while, a crazy double-fake hand-off worked, while another guy went long to catch an incredible "Hail Mary" pass. Catholic boys will be Catholic boys.

Looking back on my previous priestly ministry, I recall my first assignment in a parish, which was exciting and new. When it comes to the mission of the Church, it was almost by accident that I was able to see a little fruit. Upon arriving at the campus in Detroit, with almost nothing happening, I had the freedom to zone in on the following three areas: CCO (Catholic Christian Outreach, a Canadian campus ministry) faith studies, the Upper Room, and the Sacraments. These helped students to encounter Jesus in the power of the Holy Spirit and to receive the healing and mercy of the Father. After that I had a few other brief experiences of parishes in maintenance mode. For example, one church was sinking most of its time and resources into resurrecting its rotten church steeple (how symbolic). A refreshing discovery in my current assignment is that SBP is trying to be intentional about the mission of Jesus. To bring this about, a big-picture strategy has been developed. Rather than beginning with a plan, it seems to me that the staff has been evaluating what has been bearing fruit over the last few years. In turn, this has been systematized into a transferable process. We call it the GAME PLAN.

If you look at the GAME PLAN graphics, you will notice that all the icons are based on the red Alpha question mark, because Alpha is so central to our missionary success. Also, to be clear, this is not meant to be a linear process.

Getting people to Alpha presupposes that we are fostering a culture of invitation – where it becomes normal for everyone to invite non-Catholics, non-Christians and the lukewarm to experience something new. After Alpha, the most joyful and contagious are invited back on the team, but, eventually, all are encouraged to join a mid-sized Connect Group (20–30 people). These offer ongoing support, prayer and fellowship. Connect Group leaders challenge their members to serve in ministry and to participate in a short-term Discipleship Group (4–10 people) once every year. The latter is a place where people can gather for a Bible study or another form of content-driven formation (the image represents both a book and a growing plant). Ultimately, all are called to Worship and to the Sacraments (the image represents both a person with arms raised and a host and chalice).

Sadly, the "game plan" for many parishes is hoping that people will attend Mass. A small percentage of these might serve in a ministry and may or may not join the occasional study group. The question arises: Are we implementing a strategy and scoring touchdowns or are we throwing "Hail Marys" and hoping for the best?

What do I want you to know?

I used to think that only extra-parochial ministries (like university chaplaincies) could focus the lion's share of their energy towards evangelization. Conversely, parishes are bogged down by all of the "trappings". In other words, it seemed like parishes could do a little evangelizing on the side, as long as all of that other important stuff was still being taken care of.

Now I know that it is possible for a parish to create and follow a big-picture strategy designed to make disciples – under the power of the Holy Spirit.

What do I want you to do?

Take a close look at the different elements of our GAME PLAN and how they all fit together. In no way does SBP believe that every church needs to follow our playbook page by page. With that said, there is no need to reinvent the wheel.

- Sit with your key leaders – preferably with a whiteboard – and draw out a version of a mission-focused game plan that could work in your own context.

Conclusion

Jesus said, "See, I am making all things new" (Rev. 21:5). In the end, parishes and local churches are made new again (divinely renovated) when people are made new by an encounter with Jesus and an experience of the Holy Spirit. Once a culture of evangelization and discipleship has taken root in a parish, it can become much more focused and intentional about the primary task of making missionary disciples. A key part of this focus is the creation of a clear process that allows people to be formed as missionary disciples. When your church can focus more and more on the process, it will fill up with these kinds of people.

It will no longer have to organize centralized ministries to respond to perceived needs within and outside the parish, and cajole and guilt parishioners to sign up. It will be filled with parishioners who respond to God's call, who are equipped by parish leadership to go out and be the hands and feet of Jesus. When this happens, a parish will complete the move from maintenance to mission.

In my first months of leading Saint Benedict Parish, our parishioner Craig Sampson drew a simple visual vision statement with the connotation of process. The drawing shows a church with water pouring from the windows and a water pump pumping out water. The handle of the pump is the Alpha symbol. It's uncanny how accurate it was. The pump is pumping people from outside the Church and inside the Church into the discipleship process (the top left corner shows a map of Nova Scotia, with Halifax being flooded by the missionary disciples pouring out of our church). My only contribution was a reference to Ezekiel 47 (the water flowing from the temple).

The People: Staff and Leadership Culture

Stay with me on this next one, okay? Imagine someone asked you to babysit 30 toddlers all by yourself.

Okay, I know. No one in their right mind would ever take on this task. However, what if I told you that only two toddlers were awake. The others were all in comas. You really only had to care for the two. The other 28 just needed a minimal amount of food shovelled into their mouths once a week and to be buried should any of them die.

In my work with priests, when I ask what percentage of their parishioners have become disciples, it is common to hear between 3% and 6%. Let's be honest. Parishioners who are not disciples are not all that much work. We feed them generically once a week and only ever see them outside of Sunday Mass for their funerals (or someone else's).

The disciples are the ones who are work. They are hungry and want to be fed and can be demanding about this. They outgrow their clothes, because they grow! They get into trouble. They wander off where they shouldn't be going and get into things they shouldn't be getting into.

Back to the toddlers who are awake. These two toddlers represent the proportion of parishioners who are disciples in a typical parish. They are more work, but there's only two of them. One person can handle it.

But what happens when the others start to wake up? Soon there are three, then four, then five, then they start waking each other up. Soon you have 10 toddlers running around, getting into trouble and crying out to be fed (and let's not even talk about the dirty diapers).

Are you ready for this?

We spoke in the last chapter about three distinct phases in the transformation of a parish from maintenance to mission. At the end of phase 1, you will have so many awakened parishioners that the priest will no longer be able to care for them by himself. This will lead to a shift in the numbers and structure of your parish staff, as well as the way you form parishioner leaders in your parish.

Pastors often say to me, "I can't do the things you do because I don't have the staff you have. And I don't have the staff you have because I don't have the collection you have."

The truth is that I never used to have the staff I have or the collection I have. Both grew over time. The good news is that with a little bit of encouragement, those awakened parishioners will start giving more, because all of a sudden they have taken ownership of the mission of the Church. These resources can be used to build your staff team to meet the demands of ministry of your growing church of missionary disciples.

 Read about the role of parish staff in the section entitled "Out of the Ordinary?" on pages 77–80.

Take some time below to write down your current staff positions, then in the next column write down the staff positions that would exist in your dream parish. Remember, you want to build a staff team of leaders of leaders – not simply doers of ministry, or even leaders of doers.

Current Staff Positions	Dream Staff Positions

Growing a staff team is easier than many pastors think. The key to making it happen is vision. As we discussed in the section on communicating vision, this is about winning people's hearts and imaginations about what could be possible if …

But we don't have the money!

Financial problems in parishes are never financial problems, but always vision problems. People will support a compelling vision. It is as simple as that.

Think about this typical situation, one that I have encountered more often than I would care to admit.

> Fr. Bill is a dedicated, hard-working priest who loves his vocation and his parishioners. There is one aspect of his ministry that he does not enjoy at all. In fact, he hates it. He is not good at it and it is most definitely not life-giving. In spite of this, he feels bound to it because there is no one else to do it. Volunteers have helped, but, as good as they are, they do tasks and do not take on responsibility. Some are more dependable than others.
>
> When asked about this aspect of his work, he sighs and admits that he spends more time than he would care to admit on this aspect of parish life.
>
> What is taking so much of Fr. Bill's time and energy?
>
> Administrative work: building issues, maintenance, finance, policies, procedures, personnel issues, etc. All the things that Bill most definitely did not become a priest to do.
>
> Fr. Bill has a vision for what could happen in his parish, but feels defeated and frustrated because with everything else he has to do, he has absolutely no time to get to the things that could make a difference.

I have met many Fr. Bills over the years, and my heart goes out to good men like these. At the same time, I want to say to them, "What the heck are you doing?"

Many priests I know are spending as much as 30% of their time dealing with all these administrative issues. Imagine if they could hire a full-time or even part-time person to take every single one of these responsibilities off their plates. Seriously, everything. Trust me, it's possible, and it's awesome.

But we don't have the money! you say. Yes, you do. You just haven't asked for it yet. It is that simple.

I remember a conversation with one particular "Fr. Bill." I asked him what the total cost of a full-time administrative position would be (salary and benefits). I then asked him how many committed givers he had in his parish (envelopes and automated giving).

Just for example (and for easy math), imagine the position cost $50,000 per year and the parish had 500 givers. That extra position would cost $100 per year per family. Divide by 50 (easier than 52) and the cost would be $2 a week per family.

So… There's the ask. But you can't just make the ask. You have to show what 30% of your time and energy would mean if you could put it into the essential tasks of priesthood: to preaching, celebrating the sacraments and actually leading the parish instead of managing it. Talk about the vision and how this focus of your time would help your parish move in that direction, and use your homily to do it. I guarantee you that you would get the increase by the next week. I also guarantee you that many parishioners will wonder why you never asked before.

Oh, if you're in a smaller parish and you've done the math, it comes to $5 a week. Don't hesitate. Ask.

Who's next?

In conversations with pastors, I will often ask them, "What is your next hire?"

If you are leading your parish from maintenance to mission, you should know the answer to this question, because the more "toddlers" you have running around, the more "babysitters" you will need. You may only add a half-time position each year, but grow your staff and be intentional about it.

Discuss with your leadership team and take some time to map out in the table on the next page the staffing positions you could create over the next four years.

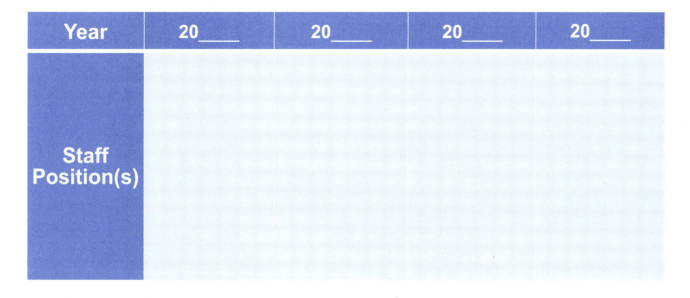

Obviously, there is one group of people in your parish you may want to speak with before you do any of these things: your finance committee.

It is essential that you have parishioners on the finance committee who have bought into the vision. The truth is that there are many dying churches with money in the bank, while most healthy and growing churches are always making the budget by the skin of their teeth. Healthy and growing churches know that they are not banks, but investors: investors in the Kingdom of God.

At every parish I've ever been in, as soon as I have enough money to hire the next staff member, I make the hire. Investing in evangelization and discipleship is the best decision you will ever make, from a spiritual *and* financial perspective, because disciples give more.

 Read about the role of key committees in your parish in the section entitled "Team Composition," on pages 276–277.

A word of advice about hiring staff. Many pastors who dream about building pastoral staff, if they do not already have it, will choose youth ministry as their first position. This is understandable. Hiring a youth minister is relatively safe. Even the grumpiest parishioners will reluctantly acknowledge that we "need to do something for the youth," and might even be willing to open their wallets for this. Everyone loves to see young people coming alive in their faith.

Think for a moment, however. What is the difference between a teenager who has a conversion and an adult who has a conversion?

I'm sure there are many answers to this question, but the answer I'm thinking about has great significance for building a robust pastoral staff team.

It's this: teenagers don't write cheques.

Yup. That's it!

Hiring a youth minister will not generate the revenue you need to make the next hire. Although it produces the fruit of changed teenaged lives, it does not increase your bottom line.

I know I sound mercenary, but hear me out.

Instead of hiring a youth minister, make your first pastoral staff hire a director of evangelization. If you put this person in charge of implementing and driving a process like Alpha, you will have all kinds of adult conversions. Adults give. Converted adults give more.

A word of caution. I know I probably don't have to say this by this point, but don't hire a director of evangelization and get them to do catechesis. A catechetics director will not substantially impact your bottom line either. Heck, it's what most parishes already do.

After you hire someone for adult evangelization, invest in another pastoral position aimed at adults that will help them grow as disciples. Soon you will have enough money to also hire a youth minister.

@SaintBP

I inherited a full-time parish administrator, a full-time secretary and a full-time Director of Religious Education when I arrived at Saint Benedict Parish in August of 2010. We also had a quarter-time music director and a half-time bookkeeper.

My first hire at Saint Benedict Parish was a half-time Director of Evangelization. I moved the music director position from quarter-time to half-time, and hired a full-time Director of Engagement (this person's job was to be a human resources director for parishioners, to oversee a new parishioner process and help people engage in ministry according to their gifts).

The next hire was a full-time youth minister. Then we hired a full-time director of communications. Then we hired a half-time coordinator of evangelization, and within a year moved this position to full-time. Then we hired a part-time AV director, and eventually a full-time director of pastoral ministries to oversee the pastoral staff. We moved our bookkeeper into a full-time position as financial manager. Our latest hire is a full-time building manager/janitor.

We have recently added two half-time non-salaried staff positions. Yup, you read that right. We advertised within the parish, interviewed and hired. These staff members do all the work, are held to the same standards of accountability, take part in staff formation and meetings and get a total salary of $0. These positions are Coordinator of Discipleship Groups and Pastoral Administrative Assistant. We also have two non-salaried deacons, and several other paid quarter-time positions, in addition to the priests.

As you can see, the team has grown greatly over the last five years, but also slowly. We have been adding roughly the equivalent of one full-time position each year.

Where is everyone?

Another common observation I hear from pastors today is that there are very few theologically trained, qualified candidates for staffing positions. This may or may not be true in your context, but I do believe that it is not the real issue.

As Tim Keller points out in his amazing article entitled "Leadership and Church Size Dynamics: How Strategy Changes with Growth" (www.sermoncentral.com), theologically trained lay people are trained to be generalists. They work very well in small parishes where they are expected to do almost everything. In larger parishes, this model of ministry does not work. We do not need theologically trained doers of ministry, nor leaders of doers of ministry, but leaders of leaders of doers of ministry.

Keller makes the case that in large churches where ministry is done by many, in order to have proportional impact, we do not so much

need theologically trained generalists to learn a specialty, but specialists who can learn some theology. We need to bring people on our staff who have the specific gifts to do what they are needed to do.

So, there may indeed be a lack of theologically trained generalists, but perhaps you are looking in the wrong direction. The truth is that there are many specialists all around you who are gifted in the areas you need and have the potential to learn some theology.

So where do I look?

It all depends. If you wish to change the direction of your parish, or simply get it moving, you will need to hire someone from outside your parish or diocese. If you have completed phase 1 of renewal, have established a culture of evangelization and discipleship, and have started to focus and align your systems, you will want to hire from within, from among your own parishioners, from those steeped in the unique culture of your parish.

Take some time to do some brainstorming with your leadership team. Let's take the latter example of a parish that has entered into phase 2, and desires to hire from within.

Here are the questions to ask:

1) Who are our stars?
2) Who has actually experienced the process of becoming a missionary disciple at our parish?
3) Who is sold on the vision?
4) Who has demonstrated exceptional leadership ability?
5) Are they contagious?
6) Who would be a great fit and the most fun to have around?

Can you think of anyone who fits this description? Write their names down here:

On the other hand, if you are at the beginning of your journey towards becoming a missional parish, at the beginning of a new phase in your journey, or have been following a strategy that simply is not working, you will want to hire from outside your parish.

Here are the questions to ask (in addition to some of the previous ones):

1) Who do we know who may know people who meet our need?
2) Who demonstrates great leadership ability in their work life or in the life of another parish?
3) Who gets your vision and is crazily inspired by what you are trying to do?
4) What specific talents and strengths do you need for this position, and who exhibits these particular skills?

Write down your dream team members from outside your parish here:

Go get 'em

When it comes to hiring your new staff, you cannot be passive. You cannot just put up an ad and see who stops to look. Rather, you should know who you want in this position before you even start. In fact, you should have a short list of candidates.

There is nothing dishonest about this. They will still have to apply and be interviewed by competent persons, but if they really are the right people, they will be hired.

The pastor must build his team. He must identify who he wants on his team and go and get them. Have a coffee, share your vision and your passion, and invite that person to pray and discern God's call. That takes the pressure off. This is not simply a human decision.

Here's another important point. If a person who would be an amazing team member is within reach, grab her or him and get them on your team, even if they are not immediately in the area of their giftedness. Doesn't this violate the value of strengths-based ministry? Well… yes. But we live in an imperfect world, and the right fit comes with time.

The leadership writer Jim Collins, in his book *Good to Great*, says to first get the right people on the bus, and then the right people on the right seats on the bus. That's it.

The single greatest thing a pastor can do is to build an amazing team. Even if the right seat is not yet available, get that person on the bus, and eventually into that seat.

@SaintBP

Within my first weeks at Saint Benedict Parish, the long-term parish secretary was retiring. I had been teaching a theology class for the Archdiocese and one of my star pupils had really impressed me. I wanted her on my team and I had a seat opening up on the bus.

"So," says I, "I'm looking to hire a parish secretary… what do you think?"

There were several applicants, including her. She truly shone and was hired. I knew that she wouldn't be in that position for long. Two years later we moved her to a different seat: the newly created Director of Communications role, and hired a wonderful new Office Manager. This former student continues in this role and is also a valued member of our leadership team.

Keeping it healthy

As discussed in Chapter 3, as your staff team grows, you will have to adjust and change your staffing structure. At some point, a pastor will no longer be able to directly supervise every staff member or even every pastoral staff member. Most people can only really handle seven direct reports well. Before we restructured our staff, I had about fourteen direct reports, between staff and key ministry leaders. It was a total disaster. I was dying and I was more hindrance than help to the poor people who met with me.

 Read about the importance of staff culture on pages 277–279.

In addition to structure, you will have to pay attention to staff culture. We already looked at the issue of culture. Your parish has a culture, but so does your staff team (and every team and ministry of your parish).

Perhaps you and your team could create your own Staff Culture Ethos Statement. This is as simple as brainstorming your actual and aspirational values and grouping them into three general categories. When you have done this, break out the sub-values and actionable items as we did in our own ethos statement, found in *Divine Renovation*.

The others

No matter what size your parish is, hired staff will never be able to lead or do the work of ministry that is required in that parish.

The primary obligation of a staff member is not to do the work of ministry, but to identify, call forth and equip parishioners for the work of ministry.

This means that for any parish desiring to take on the task of moving from maintenance to mission, the leadership of the parish must be intentional about raising up other leaders and working to bring about a culture of leadership.

Words matter. Several years ago, I was at a meeting to discuss the goals and objectives for a lay formation program run by the archdiocese. I kept insisting that the purpose of that program should be to raise up leaders. Much to my surprise, I was getting a great deal of resistance from the other committee members. Only later did I find out that they presumed that by "leadership" I meant that those who completed the program would either be ordained to the diaconate or hired for professional ministry in parishes. Of course, I presumed that they were operating out of *my* understanding of leadership.

As I have already said, we must define our terms. This applies to any parish. When you speak about leadership with your leadership team, staff and pastoral council, what do you actually mean? Do not presume that you have a shared understanding of the term.

@SaintBP

After months of working on a plan to develop a leadership culture in our parish, I and members of our leadership team were rather embarrassed when someone pointed out that we had not actually defined what our common understanding of leadership was. We pushed the pause button on our planning and came up with this definition that reflects our parish purpose statement:

> **Leadership** at Saint Benedict Parish is answering the call to influence, inspire and equip individuals and teams to form disciples who joyfully live out the mission of Jesus Christ.

We invest intentionally in leadership by making sure it is addressed at every level of the parish. Here are a few things we do:

At the level of parish staff:

- All staff receive regular one-on-one leadership coaching.
- All staff (including me) are required to be mentoring at least one other person.
- Once every two months, we have a staff lunch where we watch a short video on leadership and discuss.
- Our Senior Leadership Team spends the first 30 minutes of each meeting discussing a chapter of a book on leadership.

For ministry leaders:

- Leadership coaching by staff for all ministry leads.
- Ministry leaders are asked to mentor at least one other person.
- All ministries are expected to have a defined leadership pipeline.
- Alpha Team training is the first rung of leadership training.
- Leadership Summits 3 or 4 times a year (see page 275 in *Divine Renovation*).
- Every year we send a group of 40 to 50 parishioners and staff to a remote Willow Creek Global Leadership Summit day.
- A delegation of staff and parishioners goes to the HTB International Leadership Conference.

Leadership culture

Culture is what is truly valued, presumed, normative and celebrated. This means that to have a leadership culture, we must truly value and celebrate anytime someone inspires or equips others to live out the "main thing" in our parish. When we do this, it will slowly become normal.

Valuing leadership, however, does not simply happen. As with so many other elements in parish life, we must be intentional about it, as described above.

One of the things that we stress when speaking about leadership is the importance of having the right person in leadership.

We use the acronym FACT when discerning whom to call into leadership. One of our staff members, Tanya Rodgerson, brought this to us from her time ministering with Catholic Christian Outreach, a Canadian Catholic campus ministry organization:

Faithful
Available
Contagious
Teachable

Faithful: By this we mean faithful to the teachings of the Church. The level of faithfulness required depends on the leadership role. Anyone with leadership capacity who comes through Alpha is invited back on the team. Obviously, brand new believers, or those who have not yet started to come to church, cannot be expected to sign on for everything. High-level leadership such as Connect Group Leaders requires signing a statement of faith.

Available: Many people are sincerely well intentioned, but just do not have the ability to follow through on what they say they will do or would like to do. We look at past history and patterns to discern if someone is dependable.

Contagious: We want people who are fun, joyful and contagious to be in leadership. Leadership is about influence, so leaders have to influence people in a life-giving way. Alternatively, some parishioners may be faithful, highly available and contagious, but their contagiousness is not life-giving. Rather, they are a toxic presence in the parish. They are not on board with the vision of the parish. They grumble, gossip and complain. We do our best to not allow anyone who exhibits these traits to rise to a leadership position in any ministry. It's simple. We wish those who exhibit the fruits of the Holy Spirit spoken of in Galatians 5:22 to grow in influence, and those who exhibit the works of the flesh (idolatry, sorcery, enmities, strife, jealousy, anger, quarrels, dissensions, factions: Gal. 5:20) to diminish in influence. In many parishes, toxic leaders are allowed to spread their contagion simply because they are highly available. They are incredibly dependable and work hard, but cause so much damage.

Teachable: Every single person can grow as a leader. There is much to learn. No matter how gifted a person is, if they show a lack of humility and an unwillingness to learn, that person will not move down the leadership pipeline. Teachable also refers to a person's willingness to work with the leadership of the parish.

Who are your best leaders who fit the FACT description? Take some time and write their names below:

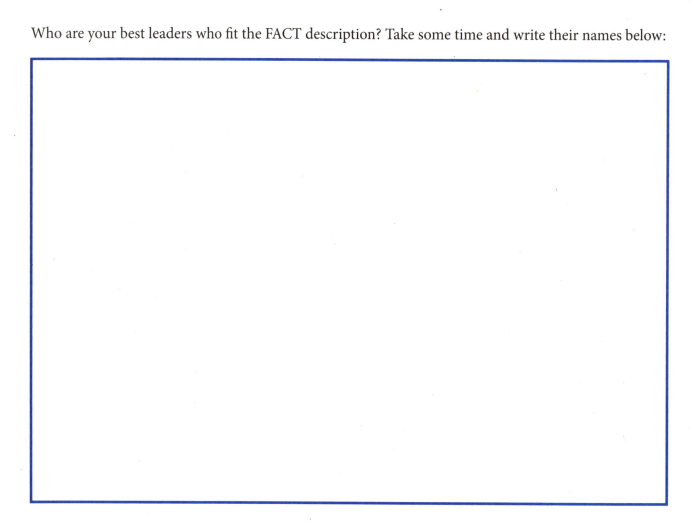

Health versus toxicity

All relationships need to be worked at if they are to be healthy. The same is true of leadership teams, staff teams and ministry teams. In churches, we need to be proactive in addressing unhealthy behaviours and attitudes at all times. We also need to be working out of agreed standards and ways to address toxic behaviour or attitudes. Every team needs to define what is healthy and toxic behaviour.

We all have bad days, but as our director of pastoral ministries and leadership coach Ron Huntley says, "When a bad day tuns into a bad week, flags should be waving. A bad week, however, can never be allowed to turn into a bad month when we are in leadership. There is too much at stake." We need to love and care for one another and our mission so much that we are willing to call each other out and help get things back on track.

Take some time right now with your leadership team to brainstorm behaviours and attitudes that are healthy and to be desired, and behaviours that are toxic and to be avoided. Both healthy and toxic behaviours need to be named. Healthy behaviours need to be celebrated and toxic behaviours need to be named and called out in love. Your common agreement that such behaviours are not tolerated is your basis for this kind of conversation.

This is a great exercise to repeat with every single team in your parish and whenever new people join your teams. Remember, culture is created by what we reward and what we tolerate. We do not tolerate toxic behaviour just because someone works hard, has been around for a long time or wears a Roman collar.

Health versus Toxicity

First discuss what attitudes and behaviours are healthy and make a list below. Then define the attitudes and behaviours that create a toxic environment.

HEALTHY	TOXIC

This next exercise is a little more sensitive, but a necessary one. I think you already know what it is. The truth is that you have both kinds of contagious leaders in your parish. They are people of real influence, for the good or for the bad.

Let's be clear: this is not about whether people are welcome to be in your parish, but about who will be placed in positions of leadership and influence. If your church is to be healthy, you cannot allow negative, destructive control freaks, no matter how much work they do, to have a high level of influence in your parish. Unhealthy behaviour also applies to the wonderful people who see their ministry as their domain and are threatened by others. All leaders should be constantly seeking to raise others up, not affirm their own dominance.

Take some time to write the names of any highly toxic and contagious leaders in your parish. This is a scary exercise, especially because these types of parishioners tend to be the ones we have come to depend on. However, as dependable as they may be, their work comes at a great cost.

You may want to make a plan about how you will move these folks along to a more suitable level of influence in your parish.

Our leadership team has been working on the book *Crucial Conversations: Tools for Talking When Stakes are High*, by Kerry Patterson, Joseph Grenny, Al Switzler and Ron McMillan. It is an excellent resource for anyone in leadership, or, quite frankly, in relationship with another human being.

The leadership pipeline

In several places in the chapter, I have used the term *pipeline* when referring to leadership development. It's a great image. The point of a pipeline is for things to flow through it. Sometimes, however, pipes can become blocked and nothing moves along.

Often in the life of churches, certain people get into positions of leadership and block the development of others. I remember returning to a parish I had been familiar with before I was ordained. It was 10 years later and the exact same people were leading the exact same ministries. Where did we ever get the idea that leadership in parishes is a lifelong appointment?

If we are not intentional about moving people along a leadership pipeline, it will get clogged up and leadership development will fail.

I invite you to work together with your leadership team and define a basic leadership pipeline for your parish.

At our parish, our basic leadership pipeline looks like this:

- Alpha helper
- Alpha co-host
- Alpha host/speaker
- Alpha Leader
- Connect Group Leader

We try to get as many people as possible to come back onto the next Alpha team. Helpers provide hospitality; those who show leadership capacity are invited to be trained as small-group co-hosts. Some small-group hosts are invited to be speakers for live talks or leaders of an Alpha experience. No one stays on an Alpha team indefinitely so they may move into leading in another ministry. Some leaders will be called and invited to be Connect Group Leaders.

In fact, we ask all our ministries to work out their own leadership pipelines. Leading does not have to be an all-or-nothing affair. Give people increasing responsibility as they grow in their capacity to being faithful, available, contagious and teachable (FACT).

Take some time with your leadership team to define a base leadership pipeline for your parish.

Use the chart on the following page to

1) Define five levels of leadership
2) Describe what excellence looks like at each level
3) Write down the number of leaders you currently have
4) Calculate the number of leaders you will need to fulfill the plans that your leadership team and pastoral council have been working on.

When you have concluded this exercise, take time to make a plan about how you could move towards making this leadership pipeline a reality in your church. Use the planning guide provided to help you.

This planning tool will be useful to all ministries in your parish as you encourage each ministry to create its own leadership pipelines. Adapt and create your own chart to

1) Define each of the roles in a ministry. Start with roles that involve low responsibility, involve low influence, and allow for higher turnover.
2) Define each role. What is required of a person for a good fit? What can be taught? What qualities must they already have?
3) Create an apprenticing culture in your ministry – not to meet a need, but to raise up new leaders and expand your ministry.

Leadership Pipeline

Define five levels of leadership and describe what excellence looks like for each level. Calculate your present numbers of leaders and those you will need for each category.

LEADER ROLE	DESCRIBE EXCELLENCE	PRESENT NUMBER	NUMBER NEEDED

@SaintBP

"Getting a Personal Trainer," January 7, 2016 – by Fr. Simon Lobo, C.C.

As we begin a new year, I decided to do the most cliché thing imaginable: I got a gym membership. Regular physical fitness has always been a part of my life, and I did have a membership at the RA Centre in my early days in seminary. In case you have not heard, Fr. Bob Bedard (deceased founder of my community, The Companions of the Cross) was a longtime member at this particular fitness club in Ottawa. He shed so much sweat on those cardio machines that they might become second-class relics one day. The hot tub at the RA Centre is already an unofficial pilgrimage site. Regarding gym fees, I have tried my best to avoid paying money for self-inflicted torture. But I have been spoiled by so much East Coast and East Indian hospitality as of late that I need to act quickly before I turn into a samosa.

When it comes to exercise, I have no interest in pairing up with a personal trainer. I can be disciplined when I want to be, and I have a fair degree of experience with working out. However, when it comes to a lot of other areas in my life, I could definitely benefit from a bit of one-on-one coaching. Over the last six months, I have greatly appreciated the parish renewal and leadership coaching that I have received from a few key people at SBP. I have also had the opportunity to spend some time coaching one of the new deacons in the area of preaching. A few gifted individuals have poured time and experience into me, and I have tried to pass it on.

In my opinion, the fastest way for priests and lay people to improve as leaders is if we develop a "Culture of Coaching" in the Catholic Church. We need conferences and big visions to inspire us, but the day-to-day implementation will require something else. The great thing about coaching is that it happens in real time. As you are working through an issue, you can bounce ideas off a mentor and get immediate feedback. Big projects can be broken down into bite-sized steps. A good coach will help you identify areas of weakness and keep you accountable to your goals. Ultimately, he or she will enable you to excel in your strengths.

The other day, Ron Huntley and I went to a Mooseheads hockey game. His son, Christian, was drafted this year and is playing in the "Q" (the Quebec major junior hockey league). He is a defenseman for the Quebec City Remparts. Naturally, Ron and I got talking about hockey – as gentlemen do. Over the years, Christian has been blessed to play under some fantastic coaches. At one point, Ron asked his son to name his favourite coach. Without hesitating, Christian responded, "Dad, when I played for Coach Dean, somehow I was always able to find another gear. He helped me to play at my best!"

What do I want you to know?

Personally, I have found that receiving personal mentoring has been invaluable. I need someone – whom I respect and trust – who can speak into my life, encourage me when I am down, and challenge me towards greatness.

We just received another priest at SBP who is beginning a six-month Divine Renovation internship. Much of the research speaks of the 10/20/70 rule. In other words, 10% of learning happens at big conferences, from talks, and from reading books. The next 20% comes from hands-on experience (sitting in on meetings, participating in ministries, etc.). The final 70% takes place when you go home and try to implement what you have learned. As part of the "learning agreement" with this priest (and his diocese), after he leaves SBP, he is going to remain in a coaching relationship with us. We really believe that this "personal training" will set him up for success.

What do I want you to do?

Let me first ask this question: Who is coaching you right now?

Whether you are a seminarian, a young priest, a pastor, or a bishop – you need to have someone you can look up to and who can push you to keep growing. As Sirach 6:33, 36 reads: "If you love to listen you will gain knowledge, and if you incline your ear you will become wise … If you see an intelligent man, visit him early; let your foot wear out his doorstep."

Conclusion

The hope is that, following through the content of this chapter and implementing it over the years, you will have sufficient numbers of "babysitters" to care for all the toddlers who are waking up. However, this is only a part of why the issue of staffing and leadership is so essential to a parish moving from maintenance to mission.

The main point is this: if parishes really get the leadership culture right, their awakened toddlers will be growing and being intentionally developed into babysitters themselves, and will go on to form their own babysitters.

The more leaders a parish has, the more influence it will have to reach out into the community and make a difference so that the Kingdom of God is advanced.

"Leadership is such an amazing opportunity. You will be forced to grow, to meet new people and to re-create yourself with the help of the Holy Spirit and others smarter than you. Leadership is a gift. When it is done well, it is a gift that allows all the other gifts to flourish. Get it right. Spend the rest of your life being the best leader you can be for Christ's sake."

—Ron Huntley, Director of Pastoral Ministries, Saint Benedict Parish

The Sacraments: The Privileged Place of Encounter

When we receive calls and inquiries from other parishes that have read *Divine Renovation*, they often want to jump immediately to speaking about what we do for sacramental preparation. In some instances this is fitting, as they are parishes that have a robust working strategy for evangelization, discipleship and leadership formation. For parishes that are at the very beginning of their journey from maintenance to mission, beginning with sacraments is not the best use of their time.

As is obvious from the structure of this guidebook, issues of vision, leadership, structure and culture are more important than the question of best practices in ministry. In addition, there are levels of priority when it comes to best practices.

Here's the sobering truth.

If sacramental preparation could, of itself, form missionary disciples, you would not be reading this guidebook. Every parish would be experiencing the joy of raising up and forming disciples who are joyfully living out the mission of Jesus Christ just by doing what they are already doing.

It is true that some models are better than others, but surely if a model existed that could deliver the goods all by itself, we would know about it by now.

In *Divine Renovation* I spoke about sacraments as the low-hanging fruit of the New Evangelization. The subtitle of the chapter on Sacraments declared them to be "Our Greatest Pastoral Opportunity." I meant this in the sense that people come to us. There is great potential and opportunity if we get it right, but what does it mean to get it right? To create a great sacramental preparation program? No!

A successful model of dealing with the fallen away, the unchurched and unevangelized who knock on our doors demanding sacraments is one that can get some of them into your equivalent of the GAME PLAN.

While I recognize that God is sovereign and can use anything and anyone to break into people's lives, this does not change the fact that we must do the best we can do.

So let's reassert the goal of this chapter, and indeed, the goal of this book.

The central strategy for making missionary disciples is what you created in Chapter 7, not what you will create in this chapter. The goal of this chapter is to create a model for responding to those unconnected sacramental consumers that will close some of the gap between our theology and our practice, and see some of them enter your process of formation.

We must be careful not to simply create multiple parallel mini-GAME PLANS that compete for time and energy.

In the end, the people who enter your discipleship process will be people who, in some way, are open to becoming disciples. Most of the people who enter our traditional sacramental processes have little to no desire to be church attenders, never mind disciples. They are consumers and they desire to pay the lowest price to get what they want for the least amount of inconvenience.

What does this mean?

- There is no quick fix when it comes to developing the best models for sacramental preparation.
- We need to close some of the gap between our theology and our practice (as discussed in *Divine Renovation*).
- We need to have realistic expectations and clearly define the win.
- We need to make sure that all our models for sacramental preparation flow into your own GAME PLAN. Remember, think process, not programs.

Closing the gap

What do I mean by this? The best way to start grappling with this is to reread some relevant sections of *Divine Renovation*.

Read about the gap in our sacramental theology and practice on pages 197–207.

Strictly speaking, if we follow the Great Commission, the *Catechism of the Catholic Church* and other Magisterial teachings, it is obvious that the Church is meant to make disciples and then celebrate sacraments with people who have become disciples.

When it comes to the unconnected and fallen away Catholics who come demanding sacraments, can we honestly think we are going to be able to make disciples of them before they celebrate the sacraments? A part of me would love to have the courage to truly move into this kind of model, but we are part of a bigger reality in our diocese and a worldwide Catholic culture that has a centuries-old practice of simply sacramentalizing with no expectations. If we cannot close the gap completely, we can close some of it.

 @SaintBP

What do we seek to accomplish at Saint Benedict Parish? What I call "stickiness." We seek to be able to connect personally with people, have them connect with the community in some way, and work with those who express a desire to take the next step. As mentioned in *Divine Renovation,* the vast majority of those who go through this process and express their desire to take the next step in connecting with our Church and its mission disappear from sight and we never see them again after they get what they came for. However, about 30% do stick around. In previous parish situations, it was pretty much 0% who stuck around. So we see 30% as a win. If 30% will enter into our family faith formation process, take Alpha or start coming to Mass, this is a win.

Defining the Win

What does success look like when disconnected Catholics go through your various sacramental preparation processes?

Set realistic expectations

Having clear expectations of your leadership teams and your ministry teams is essential. When dealing with disconnected consumer Catholics, you cannot expect a sacramental process, no matter how long, to do what only a discipleship process can do. You cannot expect it because they don't want what we have to offer. We can break through to some, but not most. Don't set yourself up for disappointment.

Second, once you develop models based on these principles, you will always have to re-evaluate and change them, but if you are labouring to find the perfect model that will fix everything, you are setting yourselves up for failure.

If your parish has established a culture of evangelization and discipleship, you will not want to put your best efforts into trying to make disciples of people who want sacraments, but into bringing the sacraments to those who want to be disciples.

The best thing to do is to create the best models, and put limited time and resources into them. Continue to make the main thing your main thing. Continue to invest in the process that actually works, that actually leads people to encountering Jesus and choosing to become his disciples.

@SaintBP

"A Little Mess is Good," March 3, 2016 – by Fr. Simon Lobo, C.C.

The other day, FJM caught me sweeping out my office and posted a picture of this "sight for sore eyes" on Twitter. The caption read: "It's about time @frsimoncc cleaned up his act." Believe me when I say that I have a lot more cleaning to do. For those of us who are working towards the renewal of the Church, the "mess" that needs to be cleaned up can be daunting. Many would feel more comfortable if everything was tidied up first before we start to move forward. I am reminded of a phrase that Fr. Bob Bedard would often use: "The work of renewal is messy!" Pope Francis said something similar when he was addressing the young people of Argentina around the time of World Youth Day in Brazil (2013). The Pontiff encouraged them, saying, "I hope there will be noise … May the bishops and priests forgive me if some of you create a bit of confusion afterwards. That's my advice. Thanks for whatever you can do."

These reflections around confusion and holy chaos have been on my mind as I have come across half a dozen "messy" circumstances in the last month. For the record, the dust bunnies in my office are the least of my worries. I have encountered most of these individuals (or couples) through RCIA. Many are divorced and remarried and others are parents – yet to be married. A few, I suspect unknowingly, have made ties to practices that are New Age or even borderline occult. Needless to say, there are no quick fixes for any of these complicated situations.

Though still young, I have done enough parish ministry to feel somewhat jaded by all the people who show up on the church doorstep with specific demands. There have been one or two bridezillas to contend with, a few customized funeral requests, and a handful of emotional parents begging that their kids be confirmed alongside their friends (even though they missed two out of two parent sessions). The fear of rejection and the inevitable therapy sessions in midlife seem reason enough to give them a pass. Almost all these people have had little or no connection to Jesus or his Church. Furthermore, few show any interest in being around long term. Most approach the parish seeking a service – or a sacramental milestone – before they continue on with their busy lives.

Yet the half a dozen above-mentioned cases that I am currently dealing with are of a totally different nature. Moreover, my attitude is shifting on this issue, because all these people are in the SBP GAME PLAN! All have taken, or are taking, Alpha. Most are in short-term Discipleship Groups and a couple are actually in ongoing Connect Groups. Everyone has some kind of a relationship with God, feels at home in our parish and attends Mass weekly. These are wonderful people who are asking for sacraments and demonstrating that they want to be in the discipleship process. The question remains: How can we help them to clean up their mess?

What do I want you to know?

If we are reaching beyond to the fringes – as Pope Francis is urging us – then we can expect to encounter more and more people who have made a mess of some aspect of their lives. This is actually a sign that we are doing something right!

I have discovered that there are two basic categories of "messy" people. Firstly, there are those who show up with no intention of connecting with the parish or with God but who *demand* the sacraments – often on their terms. Secondly, there are those who have been caught up in the GAME PLAN and are already connected to us through Alpha and other small or mid-sized groups. At a certain point in their journey, these people begin to desire the sacraments. Group number two deserves a much more worthy investment of our time, energy and pastoral sensitivity.

What do I want you to do?

For starters, when it comes to "messy" people, I would suggest that we all need a change of heart. Begin by taking the whole situation to prayer, perhaps by meditating on Luke 15:1-7 (The Parable of the Lost Sheep). May God give us a "heart for the lost" so that we may continuously search them out and willingly get the smell of the sheep on us.

If you are to embrace a Belong > Believe > Behave paradigm, how will that change the way you pastorally welcome and challenge people who show up with their mess? We have to be willing to walk with people on a step-by-step journey (*Lex Gradualitatis* = Law of Gradualism) without giving in to an approach that disregards objective truth (*Gradualitas Legis* = Gradualism of the Law). The latter suggests that there should be various degrees of law to conform to a variety of persons. For the record, FJM put me onto the Latin. What matters most is that we are going to need to become more comfortable ministering from within this uncomfortable tension.

Read the section entitled "Meaningful Community" on pages 136–144.

So what about the models?

I did say that most of us cannot close the theology-practice gap completely, but we can narrow it. We have certainly narrowed the gap at Saint Benedict Parish, and some people consider us radicals because we attempt to blend some level of expectation with welcoming.

We do need better models, and I suspect that your parish does as well. There will be no perfect model – a model must continuously be evaluated and improved.

In the pages that follow are a series of charts to outline the mini-processes you will need to develop for Children's Catechetics, RCIA, Infant Baptism, First Reconciliation, First Communion, Confirmation and Marriage Preparation. Remember: think process, not program.

Before you delve into this activity, refresh yourselves on the basic principles and values that should undergird your processes.

Read about new models of children's catechetics and sacramental preparation on pages 208–232.

When you have finished each exercise, use the six-month planning guide to help you plan how you will execute the plan with its own steps for implementation. Don't forget to plan for communication.

Children's Catechetics

Outline the mini-process for a new model of working with children and families. Make sure it ties into your larger discipleship process. Keep it as simple as possible.

STEP	SPECIFIC QUALITY	DESIRED OUTCOME	HOW WILL YOU MEASURE

Children's Catechetics

6-Month Planning Guide

Goals	Action Steps	Point Person	Completion Date	Measurement

If we do nothing else in the next 6 months, we must:

The single most important thing we must do in the next month is:

RCIA

Outline the mini-process for a new model of working with RCIA. Make sure it ties into your larger discipleship process. Keep it as simple as possible.

STEP	SPECIFIC QUALITY	DESIRED OUTCOME	HOW WILL YOU MEASURE

6-Month Planning Guide

RCIA

Goals	Action Steps	Point Person	Completion Date	Measurement

If we do nothing else in the next 6 months, we must:

The single most important thing we must do in the next month is:

Infant Baptism

Outline the mini-process for a new model of working with parents who are not currently in your GAME PLAN who seek baptism for their infants. Make sure it ties into your larger discipleship process. Keep it as simple as possible.

STEP	SPECIFIC QUALITY	DESIRED OUTCOME	HOW WILL YOU MEASURE

6-Month Planning Guide

Infant Baptism

Goals	Action Steps	Point Person	Completion Date	Measurement

If we do nothing else in the next 6 months, we must:	The single most important thing we must do in the next month is:

First Reconciliation

Outline the mini-process for a new model of working with parents who are not currently in your GAME PLAN for their children to experience the Sacrament of Reconciliation for the first time. Make sure it ties into your larger discipleship process. Keep it as simple as possible.

STEP	SPECIFIC QUALITY	DESIRED OUTCOME	HOW WILL YOU MEASURE

6-Month Planning Guide

First Reconciliation

Goals	Action Steps	Point Person	Completion Date	Measurement

If we do nothing else in the next 6 months, we must:	The single most important thing we must do in the next month is:

First Communion

Outline the mini-process for a new model of working with parents who are not currently in your GAME PLAN who seek to enter the process for First Communion for their children. Make sure it ties into your larger discipleship process. Keep it as simple as possible.

STEP	SPECIFIC QUALITY	DESIRED OUTCOME	HOW WILL YOU MEASURE

6-Month Planning Guide

First Communion

Goals	Action Steps	Point Person	Completion Date	Measurement

If we do nothing else in the next 6 months, we must:	The single most important thing we must do in the next month is:

Confirmation

Outline the mini-process for a new model of working with parents and teens who are not currently in your GAME PLAN who seek the Sacrament of Confirmation. Make sure it ties into your larger discipleship process. Keep it as simple as possible.

STEP	SPECIFIC QUALITY	DESIRED OUTCOME	HOW WILL YOU MEASURE

The Sacraments: The Privileged Place of Encounter

6-Month Planning Guide

Confirmation

Goals	Action Steps	Point Person	Completion Date	Measurement

If we do nothing else in the next 6 months, we must:	The single most important thing we must do in the next month is:

Marriage Preparation

Outline the mini-process for a new model of working with couples who are not currently in your GAME PLAN who seek to be married through your church. Make sure it ties into your larger discipleship process. Keep it as simple as possible.

STEP	SPECIFIC QUALITY	DESIRED OUTCOME	HOW WILL YOU MEASURE

Marriage Preparation

Goals	Action Steps	Point Person	Completion Date	Measurement

If we do nothing else in the next 6 months, we must:	The single most important thing we must do in the next month is:

Conclusion

This is a chapter that you will have to return to again and again, I'm sure. What is essential, however, is that this chapter always leads you back to Chapter 7. Your models of sacramental preparation should be processes, not just programs, and processes that flow into your big process.

As you continue to grow more and more into a disciple-making parish, you will have the joy of regularly celebrating sacraments with those who have actually become disciples. This is when sacraments truly make sense. Stick with it: it's worth it.

The World: Expanding Our Vision

Are you ready to change the world? I hope you are, because if you have made it this far in the book, you have already changed your part of the world. Now it's time to set your sights beyond your parish community.

We have spoken all along about how vision is foundational to leading anything. If vision is a picture of the future that produces passion in us, the truth is that unless we are feeling it, we're not going to lead it. I hope that your passion is not used up at this point, because your work in moving a parish to embrace its missional identity may be over, but the work of actually living its mission is just beginning

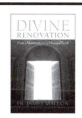

Read about expanding your vision beyond your parish on pages 281-286.

In Acts 1:8, Jesus says to his followers: "But you will receive power when the Holy Spirit has come upon you; and you will be my witnesses in Jerusalem, in all Judea and Samaria, and to the ends of the earth." The Holy Spirit has done wonderful things in your parish and is going to continue to do wonderful things in Jerusalem, Judea, Samaria and to the ends of the earth.

Healthy churches that are making disciples, bringing them to maturity and equipping them for mission are desperately needed. Some of your neighbouring parishes may have thought you were insane to embark on this journey, but a tree is judged by its fruit. Chances are that your neighbouring parishes have begun to take notice of your parish and ask questions. A healthy parish always impacts a diocese for the best, and draws attention throughout the greater community.

Perhaps, to this point, your impact beyond your parish boundaries has been more reactive than intentional. This is about to change. The truth is that if you do even a few things well, you are obliged to share them with others. If you are in a place of health, then I believe that the Lord is calling your parish to help other churches to move from maintenance to mission.

Let's keep the conversation where we started it in Chapter 1. Let's talk about vision.

What will your parish be doing five years from now to impact other churches, near and far, that will make you very excited and passionate?

Perhaps your team will be coaching into neighbouring parishes. Maybe you will write a book and tell your own story. Perhaps you will put together a much better guidebook than this one. What about hosting a conference?

You may be thinking, "What? Us?" Well, why not? You're reading words written by a guy from Halifax, Nova Scotia. Most people can't even find that on a map! Why not you and your parish? We need model parishes. Not two or five or 10, but hundreds, even thousands. We need model parishes in every single diocese. Model parishes that are small, large, urban, rural and suburban. Only when healthy churches are visible in our dioceses will leaders truly begin to believe that it is possible.

God is stirring the hearts of men and women all over the world to see the Church renewed. Dream big and be a part of the movement of God!

Remember to fight the temptation that plagued Israel with their vision that was "too small a thing" (Isaiah 49:6). Think big. Think about something you could never do by yourself. Think about the categories mentioned in Acts 1:8 as concentric circles of influence:

- Jerusalem: Your city (other neighbouring churches you can help)
- Judea: Your diocese
- Samaria: Your country
- Ends of the earth (no translation needed)

The Big Vision

Write down simple ideas for impacting other churches, your diocese, your country and the world that make you very excited.

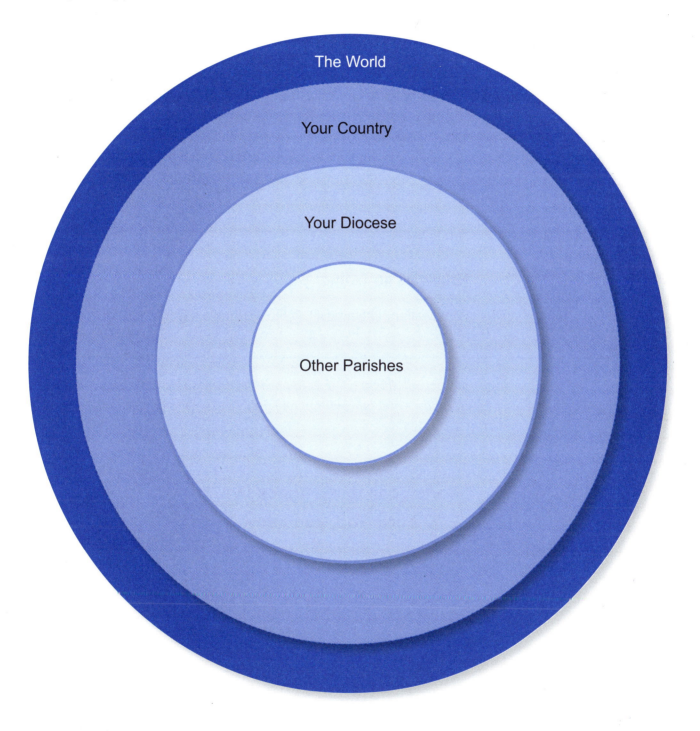

10 The World: Expanding Our Vision 211

Conclusion

Were you expecting a planning sheet to follow this exercise?

Well, there isn't one – not in this guidebook, anyway. I think you know what to do.

There is only one thing we ask of you. Keep in touch with us. Our dream is to see a network of model churches, those inspired by *Divine Renovation* and those inspired by other models, supporting one another and seeking not just to be bigger and better, but to be servant churches who help breathe life into others.

There are tremendous resources out there, as well as organizations and ministries that can help take you to the next level. You can find more about these options in Appendix B.

Keep in touch with us so we can pray for one another. Thank you for trusting this process even when it was difficult. We would love to hear from you about how we can make this guidebook better. This is the first edition, and I know that it is far from the best it can be. With your help and feedback, we can make future editions together.

Please pray for the Divine Renovation team and ministry. All royalties from this guidebook will be going to support our ministry of helping other churches and leaders in the task of renewal.

Follow us on Twitter:

@FJMallon, @SaintBP, @Ron_Huntley, @frsimoncc

Remember that you can keep track of all things Divine Renovation by visiting divinerenovation.net *for conference information, podcasts, videos and information on joining the Divine Renovation Network.*

"Mortal, can these bones live?"

"O Lord God, you know."

Ezekiel 37:3

Acknowledgements

I would like to thank all of the faithful people I have served and led over the years, especially the parishioners of Saint Benedict Parish. Thank you for your patience, love, support and forgiveness. Thank you for going on the adventure of moving from maintenance to mission. Thank you for your yes and your trust.

I wish to thank my family – my parents and siblings – for their patience with me and for their support. To my long-suffering friends who have supported me in the work of renewal and in my writing and other projects. To my personal assistant and dear friend Anne Marie Sime, for her patience, encouragement, prayers and support. I would like to express a special thanks to Ron Huntley for being my "page 11" person at Saint Benedict Parish. To the other members of the Senior Leadership Team – Kate Robinson, Rob McDowell and Fr. Simon Lobo – and to all the wonderful team members of Saint Benedict Parish, The Divine Renovation Apostolate and JPII Media. You are truly amazing. I love you all. Thank you for dreaming the dream with me and for standing up and challenging me when we engaged in that "healthy conflict" stuff.

I wish to thank my bishop, Anthony Mancini, who has been a source of level-headed support over the years and who has always supported every single initiative I have dared to bring to him. To Archbishop Terrence Prendergast, S.J., who challenged me to think big! To my brother priests in my support group and throughout my own diocese.

I wish to thank, in particular, two priests who first showed me that a vibrant disciple-making parish was indeed possible and that the burning desire in my heart was not just acid reflux. First, Fr. Bob Bedard (deceased), founder of the Companions of the Cross (Fr. Simon Lobo's community). I first visited his parish of St. Mary's in Ottawa in early 1993 and was blown away by what I saw. Thirty years ago, Fr. Bob anticipated most of the principles explored in this guidebook. I wish to thank my dear friend and mentor Fr. Marc Montminy of the Manchester Diocese in New Hampshire. I first met him when I was a seminarian, and later visited his parish of Ste. Marie's in Manchester when I was a young priest. This was only the second disciple-making parish I had ever seen, and I was inspired to see what could be possible.

I wish to thank my friend and teacher Pat Lencioni for his inspiration, support and insistence that I write this book, or rather a "short workbook" – oh well… Without the time he invested, it would have been longer than it is. I wish to thank Dominic Perri from Amazing Parish for his wise and valuable input on this project. To Bill Simon and the folks at Parish Catalyst, for his ministry and encouragement. To Michael and Nancy Timmis, for their prayers and support over the years, and to all my friends at Alpha in a Catholic Context and Alpha Latin America. To our friends at Renewal Ministry, especially Peter Herbeck. Thank you for walking with us and ministering to us. I wish to thank our sister church in Timonium, Maryland, The Church of the Nativity. A special thanks to Fr. Michael White, Tom Corcoran and all the staff for their ministry, their courage, and the graciousness and encouragement they have shown us on our journey. To Fr. Simon Lobo for agreeing to let me include some of his engaging reflections in this guidebook. There are many more of them. Perhaps they will be a book someday!

I wish to thank so many non-Catholic brothers and sisters who have taken time to invest in me and mentor me as a leader, especially to Nicky Gumbel, pastor of Holy Trinity Brompton (HTB); Trisha Neill, head of Alpha International; and Bishop Sandy Millar, former pastor of HTB and father of Alpha. I wish to thank the team members of Alpha International and Alpha Canada. To the team at Leadership Network, especially Dave Travis and Brent Dolfo. Thank you, Brent, for your wisdom and investment in us. I wish to thank John Mackay for believing in us and supporting us. I wish to also thank the folks at Gallup and the wonderful team of Willow Creek Canada.

Finally, I wish to thank God for the life of grace that He has offered to me through His Son Jesus Christ. I thank Him for His daily mercy and that He chooses to work in and through weak, unworthy servants. I thank Him for the gift of priesthood, the gift of the Church and the gift of being called to lead in such a time as ours. I thank Him for the great people I have been blessed to shepherd over the years, but, in a special way, I thank Him for the grace of being the Pastor of Saint Benedict Parish.

May all that we do be for the praise and glory of His name, through His Son Jesus Christ, in the power of the Holy Spirit, for the building up of His Church and manifestation of His Kingdom. Amen.

Appendixes: Resources and Tools

Appendix A: Resources

We have been inspired by many different thinkers over the years. Here is a list of some of the books that have impacted my ministry and my team at Saint Benedict Parish.

Barna, George, and David Kinnaman, eds. *Churchless: Understanding Today's Unchurched and How to Connect with Them.* Tynedale Momentum, 2014.

Hybels, Bill. *Courageous Leadership.* Zondervan, 2002.

Lencioni, Patrick. *The Advantage: Why Organizational Health Trumps Everything Else in Business.* Jossey-Bass, 2012.

Lencioni, Patrick. *Death by Meeting: A Leadership Fable about Solving the Most Painful Problem in Business.* Jossey-Bass, 2004.

Lencioni, Patrick. *The Five Dysfunctions of a Team: A Leadership Fable.* Jossey-Bass, 2002.

Patterson, Kerry, Joseph Grenny, Ron McMillan, and Al Switzler. *Crucial Conversations: Tools for Talking When Stakes Are High.* McGraw-Hill, 2011.

Pope Francis. *Evangelii Gaudium* (The Joy of the Gospel). www.vatican.va

Pope Paul VI. *Evangelii Nuntiandi* (On Evangelization in the Modern World). www.vatican.va

Tomlin, Graham. *The Provocative Church*, 4th ed. SPCK, 2014.

Warren, Rick. *The Purpose Driven Church: Every Church Is Big in God's Eyes.* Zondervan, 1995.

Weddell, Sherry. *Forming Intentional Disciples: The Path to Knowing and Following Jesus.* Our Sunday Visitor, 2012.

White, Michael and Tom Corcoran. *Rebuilding Your Message: Practical Tools to Strengthen Your Preaching and Teaching.* Ave Maria Press, 2015.

White, Michael and Tom Corcoran. *Rebuilt: Awakening the Faithful, Reaching the Lost, and Making Church Matter.* Ave Maria Press, 2013.

White, Michael and Tom Corcoran. *Tools for Rebuilding: 75 Really, Really Practical Ways to Make Your Parish Better.* Ave Maria Press, 2013.

Winseman, Albert L. *Growing an Engaged Church: How to Stop "Doing Church" and Start Being the Church Again.* Gallup Press, 2007.

Winseman, Albert L., Donald O. Clifton and Curt Liesveld. *Living Your Strengths: Discover Your God-given Talents and Inspire Your Community.* Gallup Press, 2008.

Podcasts

Andy Stanley Leadership Podcast

Carey Nieuwhof Leadership Podcast

Appendix B: Organizations and Ministries

Below is a list of organizations that you may find helpful. It is not meant to be exhaustive in any way. There are so many great ministries out there, but these are the ones that have made a significant impact on my ministry.

Catholic

- Alpha in a Catholic Context
- The Amazing Parish: Co-founded by John Martin and Pat Lencioni, they host a fantastic annual conference that would be excellent for Catholic parishes that are just starting out on this journey. Check out their website for excellent resources that will most certainly complement or improve upon what you find in this guidebook.
- Des Pasteurs Selon Mon Coeur: An innovative French ministry to priests and bishops that employs many of the same principles found in this guidebook.
- Parish Catalyst: A non-profit organization that specializes in providing support to parishes and priests to create vibrant Catholic parishes. They have formed a partnership with Leadership Network (see next column) and bring parishes into two-year learning cohorts. Saint Benedict Parish benefited from participating in the very first cohort.
- Rebuilt Parish Association: Mentioned in Chapter 5. The association provides excellent resources from our good friends at Nativity Parish in Timonium, Maryland, that are sure to grow as time goes on.

Non-Catholic

- Alpha International (check out the amazing new Alpha Film Series that can be downloaded and used at no cost)
- Gallup
- HTB Leadership Conference: A biannual international leadership conference hosted in London by Holy Trinity Brompton (the home Church of Alpha).
- Leadership Network: An Evangelical Protestant ministry to support innovative pastors and churches to have greater impact for the Kingdom of God. They are very supportive of renewal initiatives within the Catholic Church and have been good friends to Saint Benedict Parish.
- Tony Morgan Live: Great online resources.
- The Willow Creek Association: Serves pioneering pastors and leaders through world-class experiences and resources, including the annual Global Leadership Summit.

Appendix C: The Divine Renovation Network

What is the Divine Renovation Network?

The Divine Renovation Network brings together Catholic parishes that desire true change, seek real growth, and have a focus on making missionary disciples. Based on the acclaimed book *Divine Renovation: From a Maintenance to Missional Parish* (U.S. title: *Divine Renovation: Bringing Your Parish from Maintenance to Mission*) by Fr. James Mallon, the Divine Renovation Network is set up to give you the coaching, tools and guidance you need to take your own parish from maintenance to mission.

The ideas, concepts and approaches in the Divine Renovation Network are working. Your own divine renovation is possible, and God is calling all parishes to make disciples. Are you and your parish ready?

What will your parish receive?

The Divine Renovation Network is designed to give you the tools, connections and coaching your parish needs to experience a divine renovation. Every parish is different, and every parish needs different things at different points along its journey. The Divine Renovation Network is designed to adapt to all these changing needs and challenges by focusing on a parish's particular challenges and circumstances.

We are committed to your success. The Divine Renovation Network team will come alongside you and your parish, and through regular communication and coaching will help you implement the advice and tools to reignite the passion of your parishioners and experience tremendous positive change at your parish.

Don't go it alone. The Divine Renovation Network connects you with Fr. James Mallon, Ron Huntley and a team of coaches and staff who aren't just preaching theory, but are actually doing it. You will be connected with partner parishes on the same journey.

- 15 one-on-one coaching sessions
- 15 leadership team coaching sessions
- 12 cohort sessions with parishes like yours
- 12 conference calls for each cohort of four pastors with Fr. James Mallon
- 12 webinars with Fr. James Mallon and Ron Huntley
- annual license to run all JPII Media programming in the content key in your parish

Outcomes

- A real leadership team
- Clarity on vision and purpose
- A strategy and model for evangelization and discipleship
- Transformation of the culture of your parish
- A partnership with other parishes moving from maintenance to mission

For more information and to apply, visit divinerenovation.net

Appendix D: Discussion Resources for *Divine Renovation*, Chapter 3: House of Pain

The following is an excerpt from the excellent *Divine Renovation Group Reading Guide*, created by Bill Huebsch and published by Novalis and Twenty-Third Publications.

Bill and I collaborated on the questions for the chapter on the painful experience of the sexual abuse crisis in the Church. We were assisted in creating these discussion questions by Sr. Nuala Kenney, S.C., pediatrician, bioethics professor and author of *Healing the Church: Diagnosing and Treating the Clergy Sexual Abuse Crisis* (Novalis).

I include these questions in this guidebook because I believe that this issue is far from being healed – not just on the surface, but at its root. I believe that authentic renewal of our churches will not take place until we grapple with this issue.

With the permission of the authors, I offer it here to be used in your parish as part of your divine renovation process.

Chapter 3

House of Pain: The Experience of a Maintenance Church

(beginning on page 43 of *Divine Renovation*)

Read pages 43 to the bottom of page 45.

For discussion

Speaking personally now, how has the sexual abuse crisis affected you in your commitment to the church, your devotion to the sacraments, and your overall experience of the living Christ in our midst?

What pain have you experienced as a Catholic during the past ten years? Who have you seen "walk away" from the regular practice of their faith? How has this affected you?

Read now to the bottom of page 48

For discussion

How have you seen people lose trust in the priesthood as an institution and in individual priests? How has this affected the priests? How can priests become good leaders in the face of such a loss of credibility?

Read from the top of page 49 to the middle of page 55

For discussion

Fr. Mallon shares his own very personal and sometimes painful story here. As you read his words, what emotions rise up within you? What would you say to Fr. Mallon as a response?

Read from the middle of page 55 to the end of the chapter on page 58

For discussion

If you were in a position to counsel Fr. Mallon on how to be a leader in the midst of the difficulty and pain he has described, how would you advise him? Would you tell him to throw in the towel and quit? To just keep trudging along without energy or enthusiasm, just "to get the job done"? Or to stay and fight (see the middle of page 56)?

Fr. Mallon vividly describes a number of painful realities about our church and our experiences of faith today (e.g., family members leaving the church, and the decline of respect for the church). He states that "the first step in healing is acknowledging the pain."

For discussion

What pain have you experienced in the church or because of the church?

How well do you think we deal with sharing our pain and disappointment in the church?

Some of the pain results from a loss of fundamental identity as followers of Christ. Fr. Mallon quotes then Cardinal Bergoglio (now Pope Francis), who warned that self-referentiality is a grave evil wherein the church has been concerned with glorifying itself rather than Christ. This self-referentiality and internal focus is dramatically demonstrated in the response to the clergy sexual abuse issue.

The clergy sexual abuse scandals have brought a particular focus and intensity to the pain of Catholics:

- the public revelations of sexual abuse by clergy
- the failure of Church leadership to acknowledge and respond to the harm to victims because of avoidance of scandal
- the loss of credibility of the church
- serious consequences to non-offending clergy
- the loss of resources to settlements (and anger at victims by many in the Church because of these losses)

For discussion

- How have you responded to clergy sexual abuse of children and youth?
- Have you had personal or parish experience of this abuse?
- Have you had involvement in policies and protocols promoting safe ministry environments? If so, what has been their effect?
- What does this crisis tell us of relationships in the church?
- What does the clergy abuse crisis say about the call to deep renewal?

Respond to the final paragraph on page 58. How does this give you hope? How is such hope different from optimism, avoidance, denial, or simple positive thinking?

Appendix E: For the Geeks

I just really wanted to tell this to someone…

Several months ago, I had a eureka moment that caused me to jump out of my chair. I want to tell you about it, but not quite yet…

Stephen Covey once said that "the main thing is to keep the main thing the main thing." This truth applies to any organization or undertaking that is in any way purposeful – that is, anything that attempts a "main thing." What is the main thing for the Church? for the parish? Most parishes, to some degree, are a myriad of things, with priests and parishioners doing so many things and running in so many different directions. Without clarity about this main thing, we are reduced to seeing busyness and keeping people happy as the default main thing.

As you know, to find out what this main thing is for the Church, we need look no farther than the words of Jesus found in Matthew 28:19-20: "Go therefore and make disciples…."

Why is it, however, that consistently, the task of making disciples is not at the centre for many people in ministry? I have noted many times that if one was to observe what Catholics do, you could conclude that we have our own version of the Great Commission that reads something like this: "Go, teach and baptize all nations." This perceived mandate manifests itself in a pastoral methodology that is primarily, and often exclusively, focused on catechesis and sacraments.

Now I come to my eureka moment. It was a Sunday evening and I was sitting at home praying the liturgy of the hours in my favourite chair. While praying the intercessions, I read the following: "Lord Jesus, you told your disciples, 'Go out and teach all nations, baptizing them in the name of the Father and of the Son and of the Holy Spirit.'"

"Wait a minute," I thought. "Go, teach and baptize! That's what it says, and that's what we do! The text said nothing about making disciples."

Then it dawned on me that these words echoed the prayer of blessing over water from the Rite of Baptism, a prayer that I had been praying for 19 years, but had never noticed. I opened my iBreviary app and checked the prayer of blessing. Sure enough, there it was: "After his resurrection he told his disciples: 'Go out and teach all nations, baptizing them in the name of the Father and of the Son and of the Holy Spirit.'" We bless baptismal water with a reference to the Great Commission that is not only incomplete, but eliminates the finite verb, the very anchor of the whole verse.

Well, there was no other option now. I had to keep going, so I checked the Latin. Sure enough, the Latin word for "teach" (*docete*) is used. Where did that come from, I wondered? It must be from the Vulgate, the Latin translation of the Scriptures undertaken by the great scholar St. Jerome in the late fourth century. I opened my Bible app on my iPhone and went to Matthew 28 in the Vulgate, and there I found my answer.

Instead of using four verbs, St. Jerome chose to translate with three, by using the verb "to teach" twice. A literal translation of the the Vulgate reads as follows: "Going, therefore, teach all nations, baptizing them in the name of the Father and of the Son and of the Holy Spirit, teaching them to keep everything I have commanded you." There it was. The main thing: to teach, to baptize and teach some more.

This is how it was translated in the fourth century, and remained so until the advent of modern translations in the past 50 years (even the Douay Rheims Bible and the King James Bible translate "make disciples" with "teach"). St. Jerome's text also was lifted directly into the liturgy and, as mentioned, has been prayed for centuries. *Lex orandi, lex credendi*: "The law of praying is the law of believing." We have been praying for centuries that the main thing the Church should do was teach and baptize. That is what we prayed,

that is what we came to believe, that is what we have done, and, amazingly, that is what we still do.

That St. Jerome made this translation is a fact. Why he translated in this way is only for conjecture. I do have a theory, however.

Back in my early seminary days, I had the pleasure of studying both Latin and Greek, and I worked with many passages of the Vulgate. One thing I noticed was that St. Jerome's translation of the Greek New Testament is the most literal translation I had ever seen. He breaks all kind of Latin grammatical rules and sentence structure to imitate the structure of the Greek text, including the word order and the verbal forms. In the Great Commission, Matthew used an imperative that was one word (*matheteusate*). This word meant "make disciples." However, just as with English, so with Latin. There was no one single word for "make disciples." St. Jerome would have to have used two words to accurately translate, but the Greek text only had one word, so… St. Jerome uses one word, *docete*, "to teach."

Evangelization, which is about making disciples, and discipleship itself, have not been and still are not on the radar for many Catholics. Should we be surprised about this when the central command to go and make disciples had been missing from our discourse for centuries, and is still missing from our liturgical prayers? Perhaps someday someone will propose an updating of these prayers so that we may be reminded about the main thing that we are called to keep the main thing. I do hope this happens.

In the meantime, dear brother priests, my brothers and sisters in ministry, let's stop measuring our effectiveness by how busy we are. Let's change how we pray and what we believe, and keep before us the very heart of the matter: to go and make disciples.